*Amateur
Cabinetmaking*

Amateur Cabinetmaking

Vernon M. Albers

South Brunswick and New York: A. S. Barnes and Company
London: Thomas Yoseloff Ltd

© 1972 by A. S. Barnes and Co., Inc.

A. S. Barnes and Co., Inc.
Cranbury, New Jersey 08512

Thomas Yoseloff Ltd
108 New Bond Street
London W1Y OQX, England

Library of Congress Cataloging in Publication Data

Albers, Vernon Martin, 1902–
   Amateur cabinetmaking.

   1. Cabinet-work. I. Title.
TT197.A43   684.1'6   70-37801
ISBN 0-498-01012-0

First Printing June, 1972
Second Printing April, 1973

Contents

Preface

Many of the skills used in furniture construction are applicable to cabinetmaking. However, the construction of cabinets is, in many ways, different from that of furniture because of the difference in their use. Furniture must be movable from place to place in a room while cabinets are usually a part of the room and are, therefore, fixed in position.

Cabinets, such as kitchen cabinets or built-in book shelves, may be finished with sealer or enamel, while basement storage cabinets may have no finish applied.

The materials used for constructing cabinets are usually not the same as those used for furniture construction and the methods of construction will vary with the application for which the cabinet is intended.

The amateur who develops the skills necessary to build adequate cabinets for his home can save a considerable part of the cost of building a new house and there are many instances where additional cabinets may be either a necessary or a desirable addition to an older house.

There is considerable satisfaction to be derived from building cabinets for your own home, whether you construct elaborate cabinets for the kitchen or simple cabinets to hold the tools and supplies in your shop. If you have not had any experience in woodworking, it is best to start with simple cabinets and graduate, with experience, to those which are more elaborate.

Amateur
Cabinetmaking

1
Materials for Cabinets

1.1. Plywood

Plywood is the material most used in constructing cabinets. It can be obtained in a variety of thicknesses but 1/4 inch and 3/4 inch are those most commonly used. The 3/4 inch plywood is used for the main construction and the 1/4 inch is used for the tops and backs and sometimes as panels for doors.

The common plywood is made of five layers with the grain of alternate layers running in perpendicular directions. The grain of the two outside layers and the center layer runs in the direction of the length of a sheet of plywood. The plywood may be purchased as "good on one side" or "good on both sides." If it is used in a part of a structure where only one side shows, it is more economical to use the plywood that is good on one side only.

The common structural plywood which is least expensive is made from Douglas fir. It can be purchased as exterior or interior plywood. The difference is the glue used in fabricating it. The glue used in the exterior plywood is more water resistant than that used in the interior plywood. If this additional water resistance is not needed it is more economical to purchase the interior plywood and it will serve just as well.

Plywood can be purchased with outside surface layers of any of the fine finish woods, such as walnut, cherry, birch, white pine, etc. If a varnish or sealer finish is to be used, one of the hard woods should be used. If the cabinet is to be painted, white pine plywood should be used. Fir plywood is not suitable for painting as the grain raises under

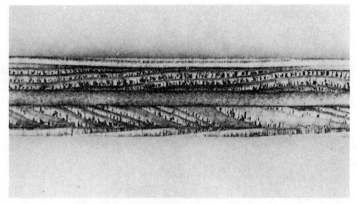

Fig. 1.1. Edge of a piece of plywood.

the paint, so the painted surface will be rough and will not have an attractive appearance.

Plywood is at least as strong as solid lumber, and perhaps stronger, due to the fact that alternate layers have grain running in perpendicular directions. It is also less subject to warping because of the laminated structure. It is, of course, necessary to consider the characteristics of the edges of the plywood when it is used in constructing a cabinet. Figure 1.1 is a photograph of the edge of a 3/4 inch sheet of plywood. The edge of a shelf or door constructed of such material will need to be covered in order to match the surface. If a natural finish is to be used on the cabinet, the edge should be covered with a special veneer tape which can be applied with contact cement or veneer glue. If the cabinet is to be painted, a thin strip of white pine lumber can be glued to the edges to cover the edge structure.

Cored lumber plywood is superior to ordinary laminated plywood but it is considerably more expensive. It is made with a lumber core with grain parallel to the outside grain and there is a thin layer of white wood between the core and the finish wood on each side. The cored lumber plywood is less subject to warping than ordinary laminated plywood but it is also necessary to cover the exposed edges with veneer tape.

1.2. Chipboard

Chipboard is a wood product made from wood chips embedded in a plastic base. It is considerably cheaper than fir plywood of the same thickness.

Chipboard is a strong structural material. It is free of warping, can be cut with wood cutting tools and can be readily glued with wood glue. It is not suitable for use where surfaces are to be painted because it is porus and does not yield a satisfactory painted finish. However, if the surface is filled with paste wood filler, it will take a satisfactory paint finish. It is also possible to purchase chipboard with special paper surfaces applied. Plain paper surfaces and paper surfaces which imitate various wood grains are available. The plain surfaces are used where they are to be painted and the wood grain surfaces are used where they are to be finished to imitate woods such as walnut.

Chipboard is more dense than plywood and it will dull woodcutting tools such as saws more rapidly than plywood.

It is not suitable for use where it is exposed to water because the water is absorbed, causing the chipboard to swell. It is especially suitable for building storage cabinets in places where appearance is not a primary consideration.

2
Cutting Plywood and Chipboard

2.1. Sawhorses

The common dimensions of plywood and chipboard panels are 4 x 8 feet. A full sheet of either is very heavy as well as being of an awkward size to handle. It is, therefore, very difficult to control one of these panels on a table saw and there is the possibility of damaging the saw, ruining part of the wood or injuring yourself. It is much safer to cut the wood on sawhorses.

You will save yourself considerable trouble if you will construct a pair of sawhorses before you start to cut your plywood or chipboard. Figure 2.1 is a photograph of a sawhorse and Fig. 2.2 shows the details of construction. It is possible to purchase metal brackets for attaching the legs to the top but I prefer to nail them as indicated in Fig. 2.2. It is desirable to make one sawhorse longer than the other so that they can be stacked for storage as indicated in Fig. 2.3. If you purchase one 8 foot fir 2 x 4 it will be sufficient for the tops of the two sawhorses since they need to be only about 3 to 3 1/2 feet long. The legs and the piece which forms the A on the end can be cut from 1 x 4 inch lumber of any convenient kind. The legs should be nailed to the tops with 10 penny (d) nails and the piece which forms the

Fig. 2.1. A sawhorse.

A can be nailed with 6 d nails. Be certain that all nails are well below the top so that you are not likely to hit them with your saw.

2.2. *Cutting with a Hand Saw*

Since the materials for constructing cabinets are rather expensive, it is important to lay out the work and cut it carefully to avoid waste. Sawing the sheets with a hand saw is hard work but is entirely practical. Plywood tends to splinter, particularly when sawing across the grain. Nearly all of the splintering takes place on the bottom of the piece being sawed so you should always work with the finish side on top when cutting with a hand saw.

The work should be layed out with a pencil line indicating where the edge of the finished piece should be. A large carpenter's square with one leg 2 feet long and the other 1 foot long is practically a necessity for accurate lay out. The saw cut should be made leaving between 1/32 and 1/16 inch for final planing. Before starting to saw, stop and think. Be certain that you make your saw cut on the proper side

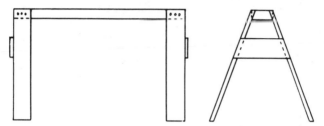

Fig. 2.2. Details of construction of a sawhorse.

of the line. Also, remember where your saw horses are and don't saw them in two. It is important for your hand saw to be properly sharpened and set. An improperly sharpened and set saw will tend to deviate from a straight line. A C clamp holding a pair of wood blocks clamped across the saw slot will prevent the piece being cut from splintering off when you approach the end of the saw cut.

2.3. *Cutting with a Hand Power Saw*

If you plan to do much cabinet construction, you may wish to purchase a hand power saw. Such a saw can save you a great deal of labor, although the final cutting job will be no better than you can do with a good hand saw.

Power hand saws can be purchased at prices ranging from about $20.00 to $60.00. The more expensive saws have

Fig. 2.3. A pair of sawhorses stacked.

features which are important to professional carpenters but are unnecessary for cutting plywood or chipboard sheets for cabinets. The lowest priced saw is completely adequate for this type of work.

A power hand saw is like a power table saw upside down. The base plate through which the saw projects corresponds to the table top of a table saw. The depth of projection of the blade below the base plate is adjustable and if it is set about 1/16 inch more than the thickness of the material being cut, you can cut right across the tops of your sawhorses without harming them. However, be certain that there are no nails or metal brackets that the saw blade can strike.

The saw has a spring loaded guard which surrounds the part of the saw projecting below the plate when it is not in use. When the saw is pushed into a board, the edge of the board pushes the guard back out of the way but, when the saw leaves the work on the other side, the guard snaps back in place. Always be certain that this guard is functioning properly before operating the saw. Otherwise such a saw can be very dangerous.

A special plywood cutting blade can be purchased for use on the hand power saw. The teeth are much finer than those on standard blades so they produce much less chipping of the surface layer than standard blades do. Figure 2.4 is a photograph of a plywood cutting blade and a standard blade

Fig. 2.4. A standard hand power saw blade and a plywood cutting blade. *A* is the standard blade and *B* is the plywood cutting blade.

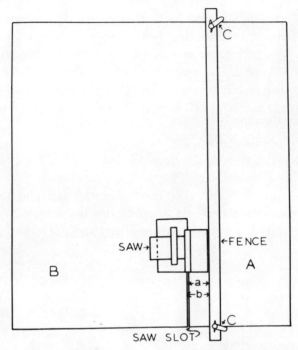

Fig. 2.5. Use of a fence with a hand power saw.

for comparison. The standard blade can be used for cutting chipboard but, since chipboard dulls blades very rapidly, I would suggest the use of "throw away" blades. These blades are quite inexpensive and when they are dull they are simply replaced. They cannot be resharpened.

A C clamp, holding a pair of wood blocks clamped across the saw slot, will prevent the piece being cut from splintering off near the end of the saw cut.

When wood is cut on a table saw, a fence is available to steady the work and maintain a fixed distance between the edge of the piece and the saw. I understand that a skilled carpenter can accurately follow a line with a hand

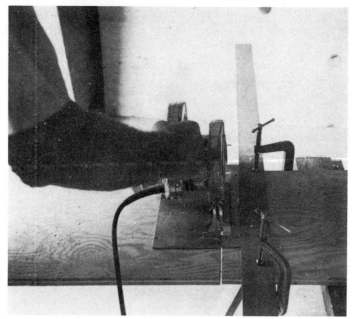

Fig. 2.6. A cut being made with a hand power saw.

power saw but the average amateur will cut a wavy line. In order to insure making a straight cut along the desired line it is possible to improvise a fence for the saw. Figure 2.5 shows the arrangement which I use. The fence must be offset the proper distance from the line of the cut to compensate for the distance from the edge of the saw base plate to the saw. The improvised fence can be held in position by means of a C clamp at each end.

In Fig. 2.5, the lumber from which the piece is being cut, the fence, the saw and the slot cut by the saw are shown. If the piece *A* is being cut to dimension, the fence should be offset from the line marking the edge by the distance *a*, but if the piece *B* is being cut to dimension, the fence should be offset by the distance b. You can determine the distances a and b if you clamp a strip to serve as a fence to a scrap piece of plywood and saw a slot part way across the piece. Stop the saw, remove it and measure the distances a and b. Record these measurements for future reference.

The piece of lumber used as a fence should have a straight edge to insure a straight cut. You can use the edge of another sheet of plywood for the fence, since plywood sheets, as purchased, have straight edges. Figure 2.6 is a photograph showing a cut being made with a power hand saw using an improvised fence.

Since a power hand saw operates like a table saw upside down, it tends to splinter the plywood on the top side. It is therefore desirable to do all cutting of plywood from the back side when using a hand power saw.

3
Below-Counter Kitchen Cabinets

3.1. Introduction

The design of cabinets for a kitchen is dictated, to a large extent, by the space within which they must be placed. Within the limits dictated by the size and shape of the space, the appliances to be incorporated and the convenience for the housewife must be considered. If you are building a new house under an architect's supervision, the architect, working with your wife, should work out the design. Because of the architect's training and experience, he can make many valuable suggestions, but the person who will work in the kitchen should make the ultimate decisions about the location of the various units.

If you are planning to build cabinets for a house already built, you can obtain suggested designs from appliance manufacturers. Of course, none of these designs is likely to fit your kitchen, but they will provide you with ideas which you can apply in designing the cabinets for your kitchen.

Since certain appliances such as dishwashers must fit under the counter, the height of the counter above the floor is dictated by the standard height of these appliances. The thickness of the edge of the counter is normally made 1 1/2 inches but the counter shelf is made of 3/4 inch plywood

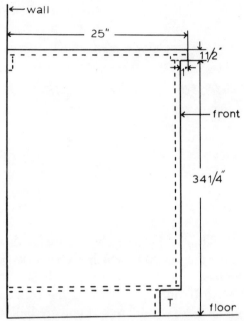

Fig. 3.1. Cross section of a typical below-counter kitchen cabinet.

as indicated in Fig. 3.1. The additional edge thickness is formed by gluing a strip of 3/4 inch lumber under the edge of the counter top. The 34 1/4 inch spacing between the floor and the bottom of the counter top is necessary to allow the appliance to slide under. The depth of under-counter appliances is such that they will fit under a counter which projects 25 inches from the wall so, except in some special applications where space is limited and no under-counter appliances are to be used, the width of the counter top should be 25 inches.

The cabinets are generally constructed with a "toe space" (*T*) (see Fig. 3.1) under the front. The method of formation of this offset will be described when the various kinds of cabinets are described.

Before starting to construct any cabinets you should make careful drawings to establish dimensions of all pieces and locations of all cuts.

3.2. Cabinets Fitted Along a Wall

In order to provide the toe space, the cabinets are normally mounted on 2 x 4 inch structural lumber. The standard 2 x 4 inch lumber is approximately 3 1/2 inches wide. The

Fig. 3.2. Method of toe nailing 2 x 4 cabinet supports to the floor.

toe space is usually made 3 inches deep behind the outside front of the cabinet so the ends of the 2 x 4's should be 3 3/4 inches behind the outside front to allow for a 3/4 inch board to be nailed to their ends. If the counter top is to be 25 inches wide and overhang the front of the cabinet one inch, the length of the 2 x 4's will be 20 1/4 inches.

If the ends of the cabinet abut against walls, a 2 x 4 should be placed at each end and between these enough 2 x 4 supports should be placed so that the spaces between them will be no more than 3 feet. The lengths should be quite accurately equal so that the board to be nailed along their ends will be straight. The 2 x 4 supports should be toe nailed to the floor as shown in Fig. 3.2, using about three *10 d* nails on each side.

If the cabinet does not end at a wall, there should be a toe space at the end. The 2 x 4 inch support at that end should be set back 3 3/4 inches from the end of the cabinet.

Regardless of the kind of plywood used for the outside finish surfaces of the cabinet, the inside construction should be of white pine plywood and white pine lumber so that it can be painted. Plywood, good on one side only should be used in all places where only one side shows in order to hold material costs to a minimum.

The separators are cut from 3/4 inch plywood 23 1/4 inches wide and 30 3/4 inches high. Each separator should have a notch cut at the top back as indicated at A in Fig. 3.3. In some instances you may have a tier of drawers running from top to bottom and in others you may have drawers at the top with doors below them. Where drawers are to be constructed, a 2 inch wide strip of 3/4 inch lumber should

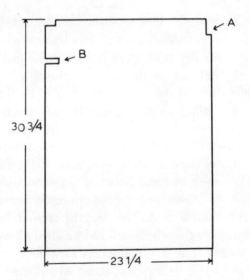

Fig. 3.3. A lower cabinet separator.

be set into the front of the separators at *B* in Fig. 3.3 so that the bottom of the drawer will overlap it 3/8 inch as indicated in Fig. 3.4. On the basis of your design, determine

Fig. 3.4. Overlap of drawer front on the bottom drawer stop.

where such slots should be cut in the separators and cut them before installing the separators. If a row of drawers extends over several separators, a continuous piece of lumber can extend over the entire length covered by the drawers. Often the design calls for two drawers above a door opening. In such instances, a separator between the drawers should extend from the strip shown in Fig. 3.4 to the level of the tops of the main cabinet separators. These drawer separators can be added when you fit the drawers.

The floor of the cabinet is cut 23 1/4 inches wide and extends the full length of the cabinet if it abuts against walls on the ends. If an end of the cabinet does not terminate at a wall, the floor should terminate 3/4 inch from the end of the cabinet so that the end panel can extend to the bottom of the cabinet floor. If the cabinet is more than 8 feet long, more than one piece of plywood will need to be used for the floor. One of the 2 x 4 supports should be located so that the ends of the floor pieces will join over it.

When you have decided how you will divide the cabinet into sections, the section separators can be nailed to the cabinet floor by driving nails through from the bottom. A strip of white pine lumber two inches wide is then nailed in place at the notches A in Fig. 3.3 so that it holds the separators perpendicular to the floor of the cabinet. Use your large carpenter's square to be certain that the separators are perpendicular to the cabinet floor.

In sections of the cabinet entered by doors, you may wish to have a shelf approximately half way between the top and the bottom. The shelf should be the same width as the cabinet floor and its length should be accurately cut to fit between the separators and it can be attached to the separators by nailing through them with 8 d finishing nails. The nails should be countersunk with a nail set so that the holes can be filled with putty when the surface is painted.

At this stage of construction the cabinet is ready to be put in place. You should first determine the positions of the studs in the wall. This may be done by listening to the sound as you tap on the plaster surface or you can use a magnetic compass to locate the heads of the nails used to nail the plaster board to the studs. When one stud is located, the others can be found easily because they are normally placed 16 inches between centers. When the positions of the studs have been marked, put your cabinet in place and drill holes through the two inch pine board which runs the length of the cabinet at the back at the centers of each stud using a No. 18 twist drill. Now, carefully align the cabinet structure so that the section separators are accurately perpendicular to the floor and using the hole in the pine strip nearest to the center as a guide, drill through the plaster and into the stud with a No. 29 drill and drive in a 2 1/2 inch No. 8 wood screw. In the same way, attach the strip to the wall with a screw at each of the studs. When all of the screws are tightened in place, nail the bottom to the 2 x 4 supports with 8 d finish nails countersunk with a nail set. You are now ready to finish the front so that it will be ready for fitting the drawers and hanging the doors.

3.3. Cabinets Not Fitted Along a Wall

Cabinets are sometimes used as room dividers. They may be used to divide the kitchen from a family room or, in some instances, to divide the kitchen from the dining area. In some old houses with large kitchens, it may be desirable to extend a cabinet out from a wall to divide the kitchen proper from a breakfast nook.

A cabinet which serves as a room divider or extends into the kitchen does not necessarily need to have the standard counter width of 25 inches. However, if some appliance is to be mounted under the counter, the width of the cabinet must be such that it can be accommodated. The counter should overhang the cabinet on all exposed sides and ends by one inch and there should be a toe space on all exposed sides and ends.

These cabinets usually have doors on one side only, although there may be instances where it is desirable to have doors on both sides. If one side will not have doors, it will have a panel of the same kind of finish wood as will be used in finishing the sides where the drawers and doors are located.

The widths of the separators and the floor in such a cabinet will be 3 1/2 inches narrower than the width of the top. The lengths of the 2 x 4's on which the cabinet will be mounted will be 9 1/2 inches less than the width of the top of the cabinet to allow for the toe space on both sides.

There are some instances where it is desirable to have a rounded end on such a cabinet. When this arrangement is used, an end panel is placed where the curvature starts as indicated in Fig. 3.5. This end panel should be made of the same finish material as will be used on the finished front. Two shelves of this same finish material, cut to a radius one inch less than that of the overhang of the top can be nailed to this panel. A leg should extend from the floor to the underside of the top to support the shelves and the overhang of the top. The leg can be cut from a piece of the 3/4 inch finish stock, A piece about 2 1/2 inches wide will be adequate.

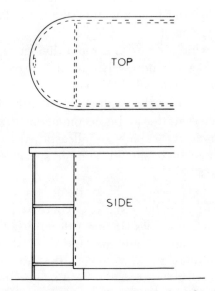

Fig. 3.5. Arrangement of a rounded end cabinet.

3.4. Right Angle Corners

When cabinets are to be constructed along two walls which meet in a right angle, the situation will be that shown in Fig. 3.6. There should be a separator at either *A* or *B*.

The space C will be difficult of access through doors into either of the cabinets but it can be retained as a space in which to store seldom used items.

There may be some instances, when a new house is being

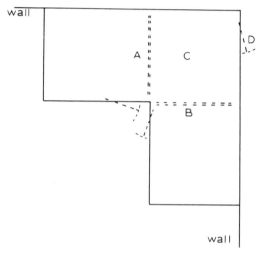

Fig. 3.6. Cabinets meeting in a right angled corner.

built, where it would be desirable to have a cupboard which can be entered from an adjoining room by way of a door D which would utilize the space C. If this is done you would, of course, incorporate both separators A and B in the cabinets.

When a cabinet forms a room divider and joins at right angles with a cabinet along the kitchen wall the situation will be similar to that in Fig. 3.6 except that one of the walls will be absent.

If the cabinet forms a divider between the kitchen and a family room, it will be possible to have the space C serve as a small cupboard for the family room which can be entered through a door at *D*. I have used such a space as the location of a phonograph and radio. The speakers are located in another part of the room and the wires leading from the amplifier to the speakers are carried under the floor. If such a use for the cabinet is contemplated, you should have your electrician install a power outlet in the wall inside the cabinet.

3.5. Preparation of the Drawer Spaces

The drawer spaces should be prepared before putting the tops on the cabinets as access to. the space is easier from the top than from the front.

Figure 3.7 shows a portion of a cabinet containing a tier of drawers and drawers over a door space. Figure 3.8 shows a front view of the skeleton structure of the cabinet.

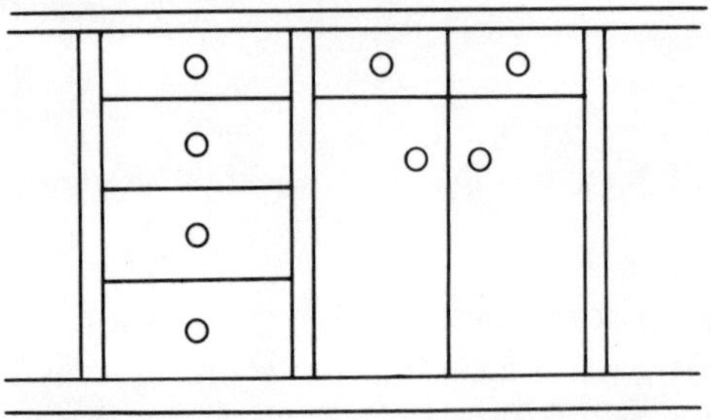

Fig. 3.7. Portion of a cabinet containing drawers and doors.

The strips *A* must be set in place in the previously cut slots in the separators so that their front surfaces are accurately flush with the fronts of the separators. They can be glued in place.

In the old houses it was necessary to have wooden drawer slides for the drawers. We now have special hardware

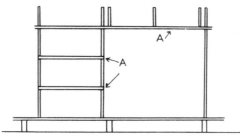

Fig. 3.8. Skeleton structure of the section of the cabinet shown
in Fig. 3.7.

available which provides rollers for the drawers, eliminat-
ing the old fashioned squeaking sticking drawers.

Before proceeding further you must decide on the type
of drawer slides or rollers which you will use and purchase
them so that you will have the special instructions included
with each set of slides or rollers. These instructions will
tell you the spacing required at the sides of the drawers to
accommodate the slides and, if the type of roller which provides for the drawer to ride on a central bar is to be used,
the instructions will show how the bar must be installed.

3.6. *The Counter Tops*

The counter tops are made of either 3/4 inch fir plywood or 3/4 inch chipboard. If the length required for any
portion of the cabinets is greater than 8 feet, the length
of any section of the top should be cut so that two portions
will be joined on top of one of the separators. It is poor
construction practice to have ends of the top overhang the
separators so that they are not supported because it is not
uncommon for people to stand on the counters in order to
reach for something and this might cause the overhang of
the tops to deflect enough to overstrain the cement which

holds the counter surfacing to the top.

A strip of 3/4 inch plywood or other lumber 2 1/2 inches wide should be glued to the underside edges of the top which overhang the sides and end of the cabinet as indicated in Fig. 3.1. Addition of these strips allows surfacing a 1 1/2 inch edge around the exposed edges of the counter top. Before the tops are nailed in place, these edges should be carefully planed to insure a smooth even surface to which the surfacing material can be cemented.

The top should be nailed to the separators and to the back strip, if the cabinet is installed along a wall, with 8 d finishing nails. The nails should be carefully set below the surface with a nail set so that there is no danger of their heads pushing up against the underside of the surfacing.

3.7. Sinks and Counter Top Ranges

The sink will nearly always be built into a counter top. When the sink is purchased, the dimensions of the hole to be cut for it will be included. The front to back location of the hole must be such that there will be adequate space between the back of the sink and the wall for the plumber to install the faucets. If you are not certain of the necessary allowance, consult the plumber who will install the sink.

The outline of the hole in which the sink will be mounted should be carefully marked and holes bored at the corners. The hole can be cut with a saber saw if available, but it can be cut with a keyhole saw if a saber saw is not available. The sink will not be installed until the surfacing has been applied to the counter. When it is installed, the installation should be done by a professional plumber.

The range cooking top is sometimes of the type that is built into the counter top. The problem of installation of a range cooking top in the counter is similar to that of installation of the sink. Some of these cooking tops have the controls included on the top surface while others have a control panel to be mounted in a wood panel at the top front of the cabinet. The cooking top, like the sink, will not be installed until after the surface has been applied on the counter. The installation of the cooking top should be done by a professional electrician.

If a built-in cooking top is used, the oven will be a separate unit to be installed. If a single oven is to be installed, it may be installed either above or below the counter but the above-counter installation is usually preferred. If a double oven is to be installed, a sturdy base should be built about 15 inches above the floor on which the oven unit will rest. Instructions will be included with the oven unit for construction of the cabinet around it. The bottom cabinet containing the cooking top will usually terminate against the oven cabinet and it is possible to extend the oven cabinet up to the level of the top of the upper cabinets. If this is done, there will be space above the oven in the cabinet to store items such as large roasting pans. The front of this cupboard space, like the front of the cabinet in which the oven is mounted, will be in the same plane as the front of the lower cabinet.

3.8. Completing the Fronts of the Cabinets

Although most of the front surfaces of the cabinets is taken up with drawer fronts and doors, there will be some finish lumber used to provide the means for hanging the doors, as indicated in Fig. 3.7. Where drawers are not installed above the doors, the doors will extend from the bottom edge of the cabinet floor to the bottom of the counter top except where a built-in sink or cooking surface is used. These units extend down below the counter so it is desirable to have a finish wood panel about 6 inches wide above the doors in the region of the sink or cooking top.

If the cabinets are to be painted, the trim on the front should be white pine lumber rather than white pine plywood. However, if a natural finish is to be used, these pieces can be cut from plywood.

The counter tops should be covered with Formica or a similar material but this should be done by a mechanic skilled in the application of such materials.

The piece to be nailed to the ends of the 2 x 4's at the back of the toe space should be cut from the same material as the remainder of the front of the cabinets.

4
Above Counter Kitchen Cabinets

4.1. Introduction

The cabinets above the counter must be placed high enough so that they do not interfere with work on the counter. They are also made narrower than the counter in order to reduce the interference and also because great depth in these cabinets would not be particularly useful because of the difficulty of access to the back portions of the shelves.

A spacing of about 18 inches between the bottom of the upper cabinet and the counter top is more or less standard. However, this spacing is not a sacred dimension and should be varied to provide the best compromise for the housewife who will use the kitchen. If this dimension is made 18 inches, the height from the floor to the top surface of the bottom shelf will be 54 inches or 4 feet six inches. If the lady is 5 feet 4 inches tall, her eye level will be about 4 feet 10 inches or just 4 inches above the level of the bottom shelf. It will be difficult for her to see anything on the upper shelves. On the other hand, there is a limit below which these cabinets can be placed because of their potential interference with work at the rear of the counter and their interference with above counter appliances. If the housewife is very tall, a low hung upper cabinet will produce more interference for her when working at the back of the counter.

Before making the final decision about the level of the bottom of the upper cabinets she should check on some cabinets to determine what level is most convenient for her. My wife is 5 feet 4 inches tall and I designed the upper cabinets in our kitchen to be mounted so that the bottoms are 16 inches above the counter. It is usually necessary to determine the height of the bottom of the cabinets before they can be designed because, in most kitchens, these cabinets will extend up to the ceiling. Fluorescent lights are often mounted on the wall below the upper cabinet. If such lights are to be installed below your cabinets, be certain to consult with your electrician to let him know the level at which they will be installed so that he can install the electrical outlet boxes in the wall at the proper level.

4.2. Cabinets Along a Wall

The skeletons of the cabinets should be constructed before they are hung in place. They are usually made 12 inches deep. The shelves should be made of white pine plywood so that they can be painted. If the front surfaces of the cabinets are to be painted, you can cut four shelf widths from a 4 foot width of plywood by cutting them slightly less than 12 inches wide to account for the loss due to the width of the saw cuts, and a narrow strip of white pine lumber can be glued to the front edges of the plywood shelves. If the cabinet is to have a natural finish plywood lumber on the front, a tape or veneer to match the front finish lumber should be glued to the front edge to match the outside finish when the doors are open.

When these cupboards are filled with dishes, the weight which must be supported is quite large. In order to insure that they are securely supported, they must be anchored to the wall studs. Before starting to build the cabinet skeleton, you should locate the studs and measure their positions so that vertical strips can be located on the back, over the studs, so that screws can be driven through them into the studs.

Figure 4.1 shows the skeleton of a cupboard with the shelves and the back strips. The shelves should be notched

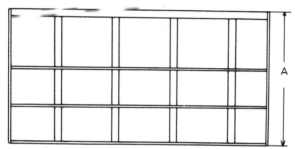

Fig. 4.1. Skeleton of a cabinet showing shelves and back strips.

at the back so that the backs of the vertical strips will be flush with the back edges of the shelves. Panels cut to the same width as the shelves should be nailed to the shelves at each end in order to provide additional support for the shelves.

Usually two shelves, in addition to the bottom one, are used and they are usually spaced about 9 inches apart with the additional space left above the top shelf.

The height A in Fig. 4.1 will be determined by the height of the ceiling and the height of the bottom shelf above the counter. The height of the ceilings in most houses is about 7 feet 3 inches. The height A in Fig. 4.1 will therefore be in the neighborhood of 36 inches but will vary somewhat with the actual ceiling height of the room.

The joint between the horizontal strip at the top and the vertical strips may be made most easily as a dowel pin glue joint as indicated in Fig. 4.2. The shelves should

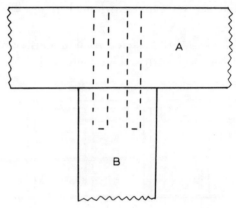

Fig. 4.2. Dowel pin joint between horizontal and vertical back strips.

be first nailed in place by nailing through the end panels into the ends of the shelves. The vertical strips, *B* in Fig. 4.2, are nailed in place in the notches at the backs of the shelves and the horizontal strip, *A* in Fig. 4.2, is attached to the end panels by nailing through them into the ends of the strip *A*. At each joint between a vertical strip and the horizontal strip they can be held with their surfaces parallel by means of a C clamp and wood blocks while the two holes indicated by the dotted lines in Fig. 4.2 are bored with a 3/8 inch wood bit, extending at least one inch into the strip *B*. Two 3/8 inch dowel pins are then glued into the holes using white plastic glue which comes in a squeeze bottle. Such a joint is very easy to make and it is very strong. When the glue is dry, any portion of the dowel pins which may project above the top of the strip *A* can easily be planed off.

Figure 4.3 shows the front of the cabinet as it would appear before the doors are hung. The cabinet shown in

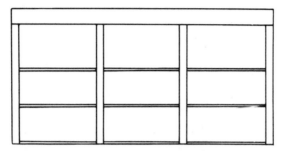

Fig. 4.3. Front of a cabinet before the doors are hung.

Figs. 4.1 and 4.3 has been arbitrarily drawn 6 feet long. Of course, any cabinet you build will have a length determined by the space in which it is to be mounted.

Upper cabinets do not have drawers and the width of the doors is usually made approximately 12 inches. A cabinet 6 feet long can be designed to have six doors. It will be necessary to have vertical strips on which to hang the doors and, wherever possible, it is desirable to hang the doors in pairs. By arranging the vertical strips as indicated in Fig. 4.3, there will be three pairs of doors.

The strips are usually made 2 inches wide so the four strips on our 6 foot cabinet will occupy 8 inches of the front of the cabinet. This will leave slightly more than 10 5/8 inches width for each door and when the two doors of a pair are opened, the space exposed will be approximately 21 1/4 inches.

The width of the horizontal strip across the top should be chosen to be consistent with other trim in the kitchen. It probably should be approximately 4 inches wide. Since the cabinet will extend to the ceiling, it will be desirable to have some sort of molding at the top. This molding may be simply a quarter round or it may be a more elaborate molding depending on the kind of trim used in other parts of the kitchen such as the trim around doors and windows.

If the cabinets are to be painted, there is no problem since there is a variety of kinds of molding available at most lumber dealers. However, if a hardwood plywood is to be used with natural finish, it will be necessary to stain the molding to match the color of the wood used.

If the cabinet is to be painted, the vertical strips on which the doors are to be hung and the top horizontal strip should be cut from white pine lumber.

When the vertical strips are cut, great care should be exercised to cut them accurately to the desired width and to cut the ends square. The lengths should be carefully cut so that when one end is against the top horizontal strip the bottom end will be accurately flush with the bottom of the bottom shelf. It is also important for these vertical strips to be attached perpendicular to the shelves so that when the doors are cut to fit, they will be the same width at the top and bottom and the corners will be square. If you do not have a power saw for cutting the stock to 2 inch width, you can arrange with your lumber dealer to rip the lumber to 2 inch widths. The lengths can be cut with a hand saw, however, if you have a table power saw, it will be easier to saw the ends square with it.

It was suggested that the vertical strips at the back could be attached to the top horizontal strip at the back with a dowel pin glue joint. Since the horizontal top strip in front is considerably wider than the one in the back, it would be difficult to bore dowel pin holes through such a wide strip. An alternate method of attaching the vertical strip A to the horizontal strip B is shown in Fig. 4.4. A strip of lumber, C, about 4 inches long and 2 inches wide, is glued to the back of the two strips with white resin glue so that it

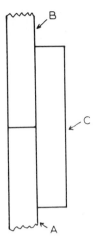

Fig. 4.4. A simple method of attaching a front vertical strip to the horizontal top strip.

overlaps each about 2 inches. Glue should also be applied between the end of the strip *A* and the edge of the strip *B*. The piece *C* should be clamped in place with two C clamps until the glue has set. Be certain to place wood blocks between the C clamps and the strips *A* and *B* but do not allow them to cover the joint between *A* and *B*. When the clamps have been tightened, wash off all excess glue that may have squeezed out with a cloth wet with warm water.

There is an alternate method of joining the vertical strips to the horizontal strip which is neater but requires more skill. It consists of joining them with a dowel pin joint as illustrated in Fig. 4.5. The dowel pin holes should be bored in the bottom edge of the horizontal strip before it is installed. If you have a drill press, these holes should be bored with it to be certain that they are accurately perpendicular to the edge of *B*. If you must bore these holes with a hand bit and brace, you must be extremely careful to be certain that

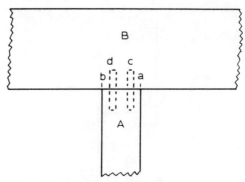

Fig. 4.5. Dowel pin joint between the front vertical strip and the top horizontal strip.

they are bored perpendicular to the edge of *B*. The holes should be bored with a 3/8 inch wood bit.

When the horizontal strip *B* is in place, the positions, *a* and *b,* should be marked to locate the edges of the strip *A*. A 3/8 inch center point marker, indicated in Fig. 4.6, should be pushed into the hole which the dowel pin *C* will eventually occupy. The strip *A* is then pushed up against it, being very careful that the strip is properly oriented when the center point marker marks the center of the hole to be bored in the strip *A*.

After the center of the hole is marked, bore the hole, being careful to bore it parallel to the length of the strip. When this hole is bored, cut a 3/8 inch dowel pin about 1/8 inch shorter than the combined depths of the two holes. Now, put the center point marker in the other hole in *B* and put the dowel pin in the position *c* and mark the position of the center of the second hole and bore it. The depths of the holes should be about 1 inch.

When the holes have been bored and the dowel pins cut, put white plastic glue in the holes and on the surfaces of contact between A and B and force them together and nail the strips A to the shelves with finishing nails. The excess glue should be carefully washed off with a cloth and warm water.

Fig. 4.6. Center point marker.

4.3. Cabinets Over a Cook Stove

A hood is usually installed over the cook stove. It is possible to install cabinets over the hood. Figure 4.7 shows an arrangement of cabinets around a hood. A pair of doors can be hung in the space above the hood. The hood should be installed before building the cabinets and if a built-in

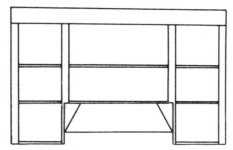

Fig. 4.7. Cabinets surrounding a hood.

cooking top is to be used so that it is necessary to have a separate built-in oven, the cabinet containing the oven can be built at one side or the other of the cabinet shown in Fig. 4.7.

4.4. Right Angle Corners

The problem of joining cabinets which meet in a right angled corner is similar to that described in Section 3.4 for the cabinets below the counter. However, due to the shallower depth of the upper cabinets, the dead corner space is not so difficult to utilize effectively. You should decide which cabinet you wish to extend to the perpendicular wall and an end panel, indicated at *a* in Fig. 4.8, should be included to support the ends of the shelves in cabinet A. This

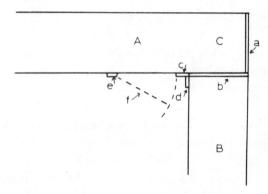

Fig. 4.8. Cabinets in a right angle corner.

panel will be against the wall perpendicular to cabinet A when the cabinets are mounted in position. The cabinet B should have an end panel to support the ends of its shelves.

The vertical strips, *c* and *d*, will serve to join the two units and make them appear as one continuous cabinet. It is usually more convenient to hang the door *f* from the vertical upright *e* as this allows easier access to the corner space C.

4.5. Cabinets not Fitted Along a Wall

In Section 3.3, the procedure for constructing lower cabinets not fitted along a wall was described. When such lower cabinets are constructed to project into the kitchen, upper cabinets are usually not used over them. However, when such cabinets are used as room dividers, an upper cabinet is often included. When this is done, the upper cabinet is normally mounted so that the side away from the kitchen is in the same plane as the corresponding side of the lower cabinet in order to avoid interference with work on the counter on the kitchen side.

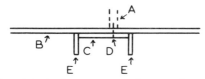

Fig. 4.9. Ceiling support for a cabinet.

The upper cabinet in such an arrangement must be supported from the ceiling, since there is no wall on which to attach it except at one end or, in some rare cases, the two ends. Even though the cabinet is in a location where it can be supported at the two ends, it is desirable to support it from the ceiling if it is longer than about 4 feet, particularly if it has doors on both sides. Such a cabinet has only horizontal and vertical structural members and it will tend to sag in the middle when loaded with dishes.

Ceiling supports should be anchored to a ceiling joist which can be located by the same technique as that used to locate the wall studs. Figure 4.9 shows how a ceiling support can be fabricated. The ceiling joist is shown at *A*, *B* is the plaster on the ceiling, *C* is a piece of 3/4 inch lumber about 3 inches wide and *D* is a screw to anchor the piece *C* to the ceiling joist. If the ceiling joists run parallel to the length of the cabinet, which is the condition shown in Fig.

4.9, it will be necessary to be certain that a joist is available over the cabinet. However, if the joists run perpendicular to the cabinet, there will be one every 16 inches over the cabinet on which to anchor a strip of lumber C. If such a cabinet is to be supported under ceiling joists, which run parallel to the cabinet in a new house, you can arrange with your builder to have crosspieces that can serve as supports for the cabinet anchored between the joists above where the cabinet will be suspended.

The lengths of the pieces C should be such that they will just fit between the horizontal strips $E E$ at the top of the two sides of the cabinet and these pieces must be located so that a line joining their ends will be straight, as indicated in Fig. 4.10 where $C C C$ are the supporting pieces and $E E$ are the top horizontal strips on the top sides of the cabinet.

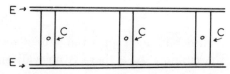

Fig. 4.10. Arrangement of ceiling supports for a cabinet.

When the cabinet is pushed up into position, the side strips $E E$ can be nailed to the ends of the supporting strips $C C C$. It is, of course, possible to replace the supporting strips $C C C$ with a single piece cut to the same dimensions as the shelves in the cabinet which is more elegant but less economical.

4.6. Cabinets in Rooms with High Ceilings

Some houses have ceilings so high that it is not practical to extend the upper cabinets to the ceiling. In such instances, the upper cabinets should be made about 36 inches high and the tops will be below the ceiling. When the cabinets are extended up to the ceiling, it is not necessary to put a top on the cabinet as the ceiling surface will serve as the top. When the top of the cabinet is below the ceiling, it is necessary to provide a top for it. One fourth inch plywood, or chipboard, is adequate for the tops of such cabinets. If you have a table saw, the ideal arrangement for mounting the top is to cut a rabbet on the top of the front and back horizontal strips, as indicated in Fig. 4.11, where the 1/4 inch plywood top is indicated by dashed lines. The rabbet should be cut 1/4 inch deep so that the top board will be flush with the top edges of the front and back strips. The width of the rabbet may be 1/4 to 3/8 inch. Of course, these rabbets must be cut before the strips are nailed in place.

Fig. 4.11. Mounting of a top on an upper cabinet by means of rabbets.

If you do not have the tools for cutting the rabbets indicated in Fig. 4.11, a less elegant but adequate method for mounting the top is indicated in Fig. 4.12. The strips *a a* can be 3/4 x 3/8 inch and they can be nailed to the inside of the strips *A A*, 1/4 inch below the top edge with 3/4 inch brads. It is a good idea to apply some white glue to the strips before nailing them in place. Again, the top is indi-

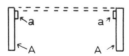

Fig. 4.12. Mounting of a top on an upper cabinet with supplementary supporting strips.

cated by the dashed lines in Fig. 4.12. The tops can be nailed to the rabbeted surface in Fig. 4.11 or the strips *a a* in Fig. 4.12 with 3/4 inch brads.

If you plan to construct an upper cabinet where the cabinets form a room divider, the problem of support is quite difficult if both ends do not terminate at walls. The free end can, of course, be supported from the counter by extending the end panel of the upper cabinet down to the counter top. This arrangement is often both undesirable and unattractive.

An alternate method of support is to hang the free end from the ceiling by means of two 3/4 inch chromium-plated pipes or painted black-iron pipes. If the cabinets are being built in a house already finished, it will be necessary to mount a board, attached to two ceiling joists, to which the pipe flanges can be attached. However, if you are building a new house, the problem is simpler. You can have your building contractor install a support for the pipe flanges before the plastering is done, and he should install them with a length of pipe screwed into each flange. The pipes will extend several inches below the finished plaster, as indicated in Fig. 4.13. When the cabinet is installed, the lengths of pipe shown in Fig. 4.13 can be removed and the pipes for supporting the cabinet can be inserted through the holes left in the plaster and screwed into the pipe flanges. The flanges should be mounted about 8 inches between centers. You should carefully work out the location for these pipe flanges with your architect or builder so that their

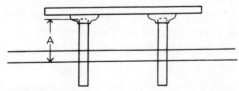

Fig. 4.13. Mounting of flanges for pipes to support a cabinet.

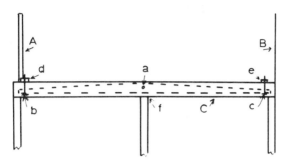

Fig. 4.14. Method of counteracting sagging in a cabinet supported only at the ends.

exact location can be indicated on the drawings, as there will be no opportunity to correct an error in their location after the plastering is completed. A coating of wax or grease should be applied to the temporary pipe studs so that the plaster will not adhere to them.

The pipes that support the end of the cabinet must be threaded on both ends and should extend down to the bottom shelf where you can attach pipe flanges to the top of the bottom shelf with screws. The lengths can be determined by measuring the distance A from the top end of the pipe stud in Fig. 4.13 to a mark made on it at the surface of the plaster and adding this to the distance from the surface of the plaster to the top of the bottom shelf of the cabinet. You should, of course, bore the holes, through which the pipe will pass, in the intermediate shelves before you nail them in place.

If such a hanging cabinet is more than 4 feet long and has doors on both sides, it will tend to sag in the middle when it is loaded with dishes. If one side does not have doors so a solid panel of 3/4 inch plywood can be used to cover it and be nailed to the edges of all of the shelves, it will add sufficient rigidity to prevent sagging.

A method of counteracting the sagging in a cabinet with doors on both sides is shown in Fig. 4.14, which shows the top portion only of such a cabinet. The supporting pipes are shown at A and the wall at the other end is shown at B. C is the top horizontal strip. The dotted lines show a beam, cut from a piece of 1 1/8 inch oak or maple which should be about 3 inches wide at the center and the top is tapered from the center to each end to about one inch wide at the ends. This beam should be anchored to the top horizontal strip by means of a 5/16 inch flat head stove bolt at a and bolts b and c extend up through 3/4 inch strips which cross the cabinet at d and e. One of these beams should be attached to the inside surface of the top horizontal strip on each side of the cabinet. With an average load on the shelves of the cabinet, you can tighten the nuts on the bolts b and c above the strips d and e until the top of the cabinet is straight. It is obvious that the joint at f should be carefully made since it supports the weight of the middle of the cabinet. If a molding is used at the top of the cabinet, it will hide the ends of the strips d and e so that the only evidence of the presence of the reinforcing beams will be the heads of the stove bolts a. These should be slightly countersunk and covered with putty if the cabinets are to be painted, or with colored filler if a natural hardwood finish is to be used.

4.7. Flour and Sugar Storage

Some housewives like to have built-in flour and sugar containers. Such containers are available. They mount on a top support so that they can slide out for filling. The flour container has a sifter at the bottom and the sugar container has an opening at the bottom which can be used to let the sugar run out.

These two units can be built into a space between the

upper cabinet and the counter. The space should be about 28 inches long and its depth should be the same as the depth of the upper cabinet, which will leave a substantial counter space in front of it. The front of the enclosure for these containers should be equipped with sliding doors as hinged doors would seriously interfere with work on the counter. Special hardware for such sliding doors is available.

It is a good idea to mount a mixer shelf on the special mixer shelf hardware in a space in the lower cabinet, below the sugar and flour containers. When not in use, the mixer shelf with the mixer swings down into the space below the counter out of sight. For use, the lower door is opened and the mixer on its shelf simply swings up into position where it locks in place with the mixer shelf out in front of the

Fig. 4.15. A special cabinet space for flour and sugar containers.

Fig. 4.16. The same space shown in Fig. 4.15, but with the sugar door open and the food mixer on a swing-out shelf in operating position.

counter. When the mixer is being used, either flour or sugar or both are usually needed so, mounting a swing-out mixer shelf under the flour and sugar containers can save the housewife many steps. Another reason for mounting the mixer on a swing-out shelf is that a mixer is large and heavy. If it is kept on top of the counter, it will occupy considerable valuable counter space when not in use and it is difficult for the average woman to lift it from the counter and place it in a storage space below the counter. When the mixer is in its storage position below the counter there will be about 14 inches of storage space in the cabinet below it.

Figure 4.15 is a photograph of the flour and sugar cabinet space which I constructed. Figure 4.16 shows the arrangement with the sugar door open and the mixer shelf swung out into working position. You should have your electrician install an electrical outlet for the mixer in the wall at the back of the space in the lower cabinet where the mixer is housed. This will make it possible to leave the mixer permanently plugged in to the outlet.

5
Hanging Doors

5.1. Kinds of Doors

Most cabinet doors are cut from plywood. If the cabinet is to be painted, white pine plywood should be used. Since both sides of the doors can be seen when they are open, they should be made from plywood that is good on both sides. If the cabinets are to be finished in a hardwood natural finish, the appropriate hardwood plywood should be used.

The plywood should always be cut so that the direction of the grain on the outside surfaces is vertical and the doors should be cut slightly over size so that they can be planed down to final fit after they are mounted on their hinges.

Most building materials dealers can supply 3/4 inch hollow core doors for cabinets. These doors can be obtained in the various kinds of woods and they can be obtained in a sufficient variety of sizes for most cabinet applications. They are more expensive than doors cut from sheets of plywood but they are superior to plywood doors because they are less subject to warping and they are easier to hang if butt type hinges are used.

Hollow core doors have a pine core around the edges that is wide enough to permit considerable adjustment of the size. The sizes that you purchase should be the first available

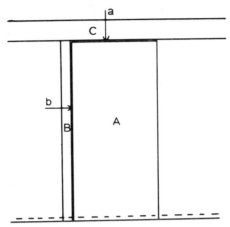

Fig. 5.1. Fit of a cabinet door at hinge edge and top.

sizes larger than the openings in which they are to be hung.

Fir plywood or chipboard is usually used for the doors for basement storage cabinets. There is another type of fabricated door, which may be used for basement storage cabinets, and which will be described in Section 8.2.

5.2. Hinges

It is assumed that you have used great care in attaching the vertical strips on which the doors are to be hung, so that they are accurately parallel to each other and perpendicular to the shelves. However, when you start to fit the doors, you may find that some adjustment is necessary to compensate for slight errors. If you push the door into position so that its hinged edge is against the vertical strip *B* in Fig. 5.1 and it is pushed up against the horizontal strip *C*, the door should make contact with *C* along the entire width of the top of the door. If it does not, the top edge of the door should be planed until the fit is as nearly perfect as possible.

When the door is finally fitted, it is essential that the bottom edge of the door should extend to the bottom edge of the floor of the cabinet and the edges B and C in Fig. 5.1 should match quite exactly in order to give a neat appearance. However, the final planing of the bottom edge of the door should not be done until after the door has been hung on its hinges.

There are a number of kinds of hinges that can be used for hanging cabinet doors. The choice depends on the appearance desired. Some people prefer ornamental hinges while others prefer butt hinges which are quite unobtrusive.

The simplest hinges to apply are those which are attached on the surface as indicated in Fig. 5.2. These hinges are made in a variety of shapes and materials. They may be copper finish, brass finish or chromium plated. Such hinges are easy to install and are often used on storage cabinets where appearance is not particularly important. There are also many instances where hinges of this type are used for ornamental reasons. When such hinges are used, they should first be attached to the door. Two hinges are used for each door and they are placed about three inches from the top and bottom. The actual distance will depend on the shape of the hinge. The hinges should be so placed that the center of the hinge pin is at the edge of the door and the pin should be accurately parallel to the edge of the door. The locations of the screw holes should be carefully marked with a sharp pencil while the hinge is held in its proper position. The screw holes should be drilled with the proper size drill for the screws that will be used. Most cabinet hinges are attached with No. 6 wood screws and a No. 36 drill will make the proper size hole.

After the hinges are attached to the door, it should be pushed in place with pieces of cardboard, not more than 1/32 inch thick, at the edges a and b in Fig. 5.1 and, while it

Fig. 5.2. Application of a surface hinge.

is firmly held in place, the locations of the screw holes in part *B* of Fig. 5.1 should be marked. Drill the holes for the screws, remove the pieces of cardboard and drive in the screws. The door should now swing freely and close with gaps of not more than 1/32 inch at *a* and *b* in Fig. 5.1.

Butt hinges are more commonly used than surface hinges on cabinets such as kitchen cabinets. Figure 5.3 shows how such hinges are attached. If the hinge is simply attached to the surface, the gap at *b* in Fig. 5.1 will be nearly 1/8 inch when the door is closed. In order to eliminate this gap, the hinge must be mortised into the edges of the door and the vertical strip to which it is hinged by an amount equal to or slightly less than the thickness of the hinge material. This is done by marking the area to be covered by the hinge and cutting out the mortise with a sharp chisel. This must be done with great care. If the mortise is not cut deeply enough, an ugly gap will be present when the door is closed. It is even more serious to make the mortise too deep. This will

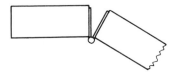

Fig. 5.3. Application of a simple butt hinge.

cause the edge of the door and the edge of the vertical strip to contact before the door is closed and if it is forced shut there will be a tendency to pull the screws out of the wood.

Both hinges should be mortised into the edge of the door and the position of the mortise in the upright B in Fig. 5.1 for the top hinge should be located by measurement and the locations of the screw holes can be marked with a sharp pencil. This hinge should be so located that the door clear-

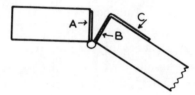

Fig. 5.4. Special butt hinge for a plywood door.

ance at the top will be about 1/32 inch. After the screw holes are drilled, remove the pin from the hinge and attach the free part of the hinge to the upright B. After this part of the hinge is attached, put the door in place again and replace the hinge pin.

Hold the door in its proper position being careful not to put any excessive strain on the hinge screws and mark the position for the mortise for the bottom hinge. Remove the pin from the top hinge again so that you can put the door aside and cut the mortise for the lower hinge. The door should again be put in position and the top hinge pin reinserted so you can mark and drill the screw holes for the lower hinge.

The problem of mounting butt hinges on plywood edges is difficult because of the difference in direction of the grain of the wood in the alternate layers of the plywood. This makes it difficult to drill the screw holes for the hinges in the proper positions. If the upright B can be made from regular lumber instead of plywood, a type of butt hinge is available which will eliminate this difficulty. These hinges are made as indicated in Fig. 5.4. The side A of the hinge is attached to the upright B in Fig. 5.1 and the side B in Fig. 5.4 is attached to the plywood door. The portion C of the hinge is attached to the back surface of the door and is not mortised into the door. The part B is mortised into the edge of the door. Due to the fact that the part C is attached to the surface of the plywood, the screw holes can be accurately located and they should be located, the holes drilled and the screws driven in tightly before the screw hole in the part B is located and drilled.

The attachment of the portion A to the vertical upright is accomplished in the same manner as that with the simple butt hinges.

When either type of butt hinge is used, there are apt to be occasions when the mortises will be cut too deeply. This will be immediately evident when you attempt to close the door. Do not force it shut as a severe strain will be applied to the hinge screws. A professional carpenter describes this condition as "hinge bound." If your cabinet door is hinge bound, you can determine which hinge is at fault by loosening the screws on first one hinge and then the other. When you determine which hinge is causing the binding, the problem can be corrected if you will cut a piece of cardboard to the shape of the portion of the hinge attached to the vertical strip, cut holes for the screws and place the piece of cardboard in the mortise back of the hinge.

If the mortises are not cut deeply enough, the gap at b in Fig. 5.1 will be too wide. If the depths of the mortises for the two hinges are not the same, the gaps at a and b in Fig. 5.1 will vary along their lengths. These conditions can be readily corrected by removing the hinges and cut-

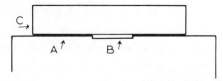

Fig. 5.5. Method for checking the depth of a hinge mortise.

ting away some more wood in the mortise that is too shallow, or by adding a piece of cardboard behind the hinge in the mortise which is too deep. After you have hung a few doors with butt hinges, you will gain the necessary experience to cut these mortises quite accurately. A method for checking the mortises for proper depth is shown in Fig. 5.5. A is the edge of the upright or door in which the mortise is being cut, B is the hinge and C is a straight edge such as a steel scale. The depth of the mortise should be such that when the straight edge is placed as indicated in Fig. 5.5 and pressed down tightly it will just clear the edge A.

If there is only one door in the opening and the door was cut slightly over size, Fig. 5.6 shows the condition when the door is closed. The hinges are on the edge A and the door will interfere with the upright B. If a pencil line is drawn the length of the upright at C, the amount of wood which must be removed from the edge of the door can be determined by measuring the distance from the line C to the edge of B. The door can be removed by removing the pins from the hinges and the edge can be planed until it will close with a gap at C of about 1/32 inch.

If the space is closed by a pair of doors, one door can be closed and the other door can be closed against it in the manner shown in Fig. 5.6. The mark C shows the amount that should be planed off from the door B in order for the doors to close without interfering. The gap between the doors should be approximately 1/32 inch.

The bottom edge of the doors should now be planed so that they are flush with the bottom of the vertical uprights. If a straight edge is held so that it is flush with the bottom ends of the vertical uprights on the two sides, a fine pencil line can be drawn across the door or doors and the bottom edges can be planed to the pencil line. The edges can be planed with either a hand plane or a jointer.

Fig. 5.6. Method of checking for the final fit of the door.

5.3. Cabinet Door Pulls

It is necessary to have some sort of pull for opening cabinet doors. There is a great variety of pulls available and the choice will depend on the kind of cabinet and the decorative effect desired. If ornamental hinges are used, the pulls should be chosen to match the hinges.

The door pulls may be of the handle type or knobs. Handle type pulls are usually used with ornamental hinges. If knobs are used, they may be simple wood knobs or decorative metal knobs. If chromium plated hinges are used, the knobs or handles should be chromium plated.

Kitchen cabinets are opened and closed many more times per day than any other kind of cabinets around the house. When the cabinet is opened there is a slight tendency for the fingernails of the person opening the cabinet to scrape the surface of the wood below the pull. For this reason, it is desirable to choose knobs which are installed with a circular metal plate between them and the wood surface for kitchen cabinets. This is not an important consideration for other

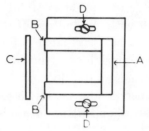

Fig. 5.7. Magnetic door catch.

cabinets in the house which are usually opened only a few times per week.

Wood knobs are less expensive than metal knobs or handles and are therefore usually used for storage cabinets where appearance is not a factor. There are, however, instances where wood knobs are used where appearance is an important factor. Wood knobs can be painted or stained to match the rest of the cabinet and are, therefore, used in places where it is desirable to have the knobs unobtrusive.

5.4. Cabinet Door Catches

The three most common types of cabinet door catches are magnetic, spring roller and snap grip spring catches.

Magnetic catches vary in shape but they all operate on

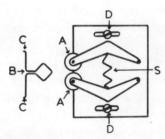

Fig. 5.8. Spring roller type door catch.

the principle illustrated in Fig. 5.7, where A is a permanent magnet, BB are iron legs and C is an iron strip. The unit consisting of A and BB is attached to a shelf in the cabinet and the iron strip C is attached to the door. When the cabinet door is closed, the strip C makes contact with the legs BB, closing the magnetic circuit. When the magnetic circuit is closed through the iron strip C, it is firmly attracted to the legs and will hold the door closed. The unit containing the magnet and the two iron legs is mounted on a base which is attached to a shelf with the screws DD. The screw holes are slots permitting about 1/2 inch range of adjust ment of the position of the magnetic element. It should be so adjusted that the iron strip C just contacts the legs BI when the door is closed.

The spring roller type of catch is illustrated in Fig. 5.8 The rollers A are usually made of a plastic material and ar held together by the spring S. The unit containing the roll ers is mounted on a cabinet shelf with the screws DD throug slotted holes to permit adjustment of the unit. It is necessa to mount the catch B, which is held by the rollers when th door is closed, quite accurately on the door. In order to this, the unit containing the rollers is first mounted on a sh and, with the catch B held between the rollers, the door closed against it. The catch has a point C at each corner a when the door is closed against it the points will mark door to indicate the proper location of the catch B. The ca can then be attached to the door with two screws. After catch is attached to the door the unit is adjusted on shelf until the rollers will just grasp the catch when the d is closed.

The snap grip spring catch is similar to the spring ro catch except that a pair of metal wedges replace the pla rollers.

When Cabinet door catches are installed, it is desira

whenever possible, to install them on the bottom of one of the shelves rather than on the top surface of the shelf in order to avoid interference with use of the shelf.

5.5. Cabinet Door Locks

Most cabinets do not require locks. There are, however, instances where cabinets are intended to store materials such as pesticides or guns which could be a source of danger if children could gain access to them. Such cabinets should be equipped with locks.

There are two types of locks which can conveniently be applied to cabinet doors. Both types are applied to the back of the door and usually some wood must be cut away for the lock to be fitted.

One of these types requires a hole to be bored through the door to accept a cylinder which projects through to the front of the door. The keyhole is in the end of the cylinder which shows at the front of the door. Some locks of this type do not require any cutting of the wood on the door except to bore the hole for the cylinder.

The second type of lock requires a hole to be cut to accept a key which is inserted through the wood of the door into the lock at the back. Since it is difficult to make a nice-looking hole for a key, a keyhole escutcheon plate is usually used to cover the area of the key hole in the wood.

In instances where such simple locks are used it is usually necessary simply to mark the place where the bolt strikes the wood on the edge of the vertical upright and cut a rectangular hole in the wood to accept the bolt.

When a lock more secure than the simple bolt type lock is needed, a hinge type hasp can be used so that the door can be locked with a padlock.

6
Making and Fitting Drawers

6.1. Introduction

Many kinds of drawers are used in cabinets and there are several types of construction depending on the application and the tools available for constructing them.

Roller type drawer slides are usually used on kitchen cabinet drawers and instructions for the proper fitting of the drawers are furnished with the drawer slides. However, the way in which the drawers are actually constructed will depend on the tools available for constructing them.

In my book *Amateur Furniture Construction* I have described in detail how to construct drawers which are assembled with dovetail joints. There is no reason why cabinet drawers cannot be constructed using dovetail joints. However, they are usually not used in cabinet construction.

White pine lumber is usually used for the sides and backs of cabinet drawers. If the cabinet is to be painted, white pine lumber is also used for the fronts. If the front of the cabinet is constructed of hardwood plywood, the drawer fronts will need to be made from this same plywood. When the drawer fronts are to be made from plywood, they are usually designed to close flush with the front of the cabinet

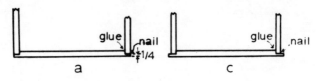

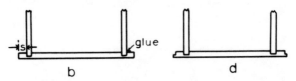

Fig. 6.1. Methods of attaching the sides to the front of a cabinet drawer.

    a. A drawer which does not use side mounted roller slides and does not have a lip.

    b. A drawer which is to use side mounted roller slides and does not have a lip.

    c. A drawer which does not use side mounted roller slides but has a lip.

    d. A drawer which is to use side mounted roller slides and has a lip.

because the edge grain of the plywood would show around the lip and it is difficult to finish the plywood edge grain to match the surface of the plywood.

There is an advantage in constructing the drawers with a lip because the fit of the drawer is not as critical. It is important to have the fit of the drawer loose enough so it will not stick in damp weather. If the drawers are constructed during the winter, sufficient allowance must be made for the swelling which will take place during damp weather in the summer. Usually about 1/16 inch allowance will be sufficient. Remember that the wood will expand considerably more across the grain than parallel to the grain when it swells due to dampness. You should use great care in fitting the drawers as there is probably nothing more aggravating than a sticking drawer and it is a condition difficult to correct after the drawer is constructed. It is also important to assemble the drawer with square corners, particularly if it is a flush drawer, or the drawer will not close so that it is flush at both ends of the front.

6.2. Attaching the Drawer Sides to the Front and Back

Drawers, such as those used in kitchen cabinets, usually close flush with the front of the cabinet and the frame serves as a stop for the drawer front as indicated in Fig. 3.4. However, it is also possible to construct such drawers with a lip if such construction is desired. The lip will then stop against the outside of the cabinet front.

If you have a power saw with a dado cutter available the problem of constructing the drawers is greatly simplified.

Figure 6.1 shows methods of attaching the drawer sides to the front. Figure 6.1 *a* shows the method of attaching the sides to the front for a flush drawer which does not use side mounted drawer slides. Figure 6.1 *b* shows a method of attaching the sides to the front when side mounted drawer slides are used. The dimension *s* is the width required for

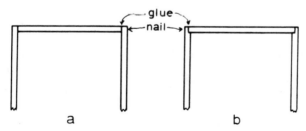

Fig. 6.2. Methods of attaching the back to the sides of a drawer.

the drawer slide plus the overlap on the drawer frame (see Fig. 3.4). Usually *s* will be equal to the width required for the drawer slide plus 3/8 inch. Figure 6.1 *c* shows the method of attaching the sides to a drawer front which has a lip and does not have side-mounted drawer slides. The lip is usually made to overlap the front of the cabinet 1/4 inch. Figure 6.1 *d* shows the method of construction of the drawer front if side mounted drawer slides are used and the drawer front is to have a lip. The sides may be made of 1/2 inch or 3/4 inch lumber and the rabbet is usually made 1/2 inch deep, leaving the thickness of the lip equal to 1/4 inch. The sides may be attached with glue and in the examples shown in Figs. 6.1 *a* and 6.1 *c* the sides should be nailed to the front with 6 d finishing nails.

If a power saw is not available, you can make the necessary cuts for the methods of attaching the sides shown in

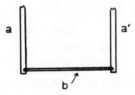

Fig. 6.3. A method of mounting the bottom in a drawer.

Figs. 6.1 *a* and *b* with a back saw. The wood between the cuts in Fig. 6.1 *b* can be removed with a chisel.

It is not feasible to cut the rabbet for the lip on the top and bottom of a drawer with a hand saw unless the drawer is very narrow. It is, however, possible to purchase a rabbeting plane which can be used to cut the rabbet for the lip.

Since the back of the drawer does not extend beyond the sides, its attachment is relatively simple. In most instances, the arrangement shown in Fig. 6.2 *a* is adequate. Glue is applied to the surfaces of the back and sides and the sides are nailed to the back as indicated in Fig. 6.2 *a*. The arrangement shown in Fig. 6.2 *b* is somewhat stronger than that in Fig. 6.2 *a* because of the increased surface available for glue. If adequate tools for cutting the rabbets at the ends of the drawer sides are not available, the construction shown in Fig. 6.2 *a* is preferable.

6.3. Drawer Bottoms

The drawer bottoms may be cut from 1/4 inch plywood or either 1/8 or 1/4 inch hardboard. One-fourth inch hardboard would be used only in very large drawers.

The best method of mounting the bottom is that shown in Fig. 6.3 where *b* is the bottom and *a* and *a'* are the sides or ends of the drawer. This method may be used with drawer sides of either 1/2 inch or 3/4 inch lumber. The slots in which the edges of the bottom fit should be cut 1/4 inch deep and the width of the slots should be such that it is not necessary to use force to push the edge of the bottom into the slot. The bottom edge of the slot should be approximately 1/4 inch above the bottom of the sides and back of the drawer. Since the bottom edge of the front will sometimes be lower than the bottom edge of the sides, the distance from the bottom of the front to the bottom of the slot will be greater than the corresponding distance on the sides and back. It is important that these slots in the sides, back and front be properly located so that they will match when the drawer is assembled.

Of course, you will not be able to cut the slots indicated in Fig. 6.3 if you do not have a power saw. If a power saw is not available to you, there is an alternate method of mounting the bottom indicated in Fig. 6.4. If you can

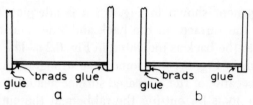

Fig. 6.4. An alternate method of mounting the bottom in a drawer.

obtain 1/4 inch quarter round, it can be attached to the sides and ends with brads and glue as indicated in Fig. 6.4 *a.* If 1/4 inch quarter round is not available, you can have your lumber dealer cut 1/4 inch square strips in his mill and pieces can be cut and attached with brads and glue as indicated in Fig. 6.4 *b.*

If the drawer sides and ends are prepared with slots as indicated in Fig. 6.3, the bottom should be cut slightly less than 1/2 inch longer and wider than the inside dimensions of the drawer and the drawer is assembled by attaching the front and back to one of the sides. Some glue is applied in the slots of the front, back and side and the bottom is pushed into place. After the bottom is pushed into place, glue is applied to the slot of the second side and it is attached. Check the corners of the drawer with a small square to be certain that they are square. If the drawer is prepared as indicated in Fig. 6.4, the bottom should be cut to the same dimensions as the inside of the drawer, the sides and ends are assembled and, after glue is applied to the tops of the quarter round or the square strips, the bottom is pushed down on top of them and a weight is applied to the bottom and left until the glue has set. White glue, which is available ready-to-use in squeeze bottles, is very convenient and entirely satisfactory. Excess glue which is squeezed out should be wiped off with a wet cloth or paper towel. Do not apply so much weight to the bottom that it is deflected out of shape. It is important to cut the bottoms accurately to the proper dimensions because, when the drawer is assembled with the bottom in slots in the sides and ends as indicated in Fig. 6.3, the bottom can be a means of forcing the drawer into a perfectly rectangular shape. If the drawer is assembled as in Fig. 6.4, it should be assembled without the bottom. Be certain that the corners are square, and the bottom can then be installed after the glue at the corners has set.

6.4. Drawer Slides and Guides

If roller type slides are to be used, you should follow the instructions accompanying the slides for fitting the drawer. If roller type slides are not to be used, wood slides must be made of a hard wood such as maple or birch. If the sides of the opening are not flush with the sides of the space within which the drawer operates, an L-shaped drawer slide like that shown in Fig. 6.5 should be constructed. The width of the edge *a*, in Fig. 6.5, is such that it will fill the space between the inside edge of the drawer opening and the wall of the space in which the drawer slides. The edge *c* serves as a guide for the edge of the drawer side and should be at least 1/2 inch high. The edge *b* is the surface on which the bottom edge of the side of the drawer slides. This edge should be at least 1/2 inch if 1/2 inch lumber is used for the side of the drawer, and if 3/4 inch lumber is used for the side of the drawer, the edge *b* should be 3/4 inch. If power tools are available, this slide can be fabricated from a single piece of lumber, but it can be made of two pieces joined along the dotted line *d* in Fig. 6.5. The slide can be anchored to the side of the drawer cavity by means of screws *e*.

If the width of the cavity for the drawer is the same as the width of the opening, the sides of the opening will serve as the side guides for the drawer and it is simply necessary to provide slides for the bottom edges of the drawer sides. Such a slide is shown in Fig. 6.6. The surface

Fig. 6.5. An L-shaped drawer slide.

a is the surface on which the drawer slides, *b* is the wall of the cavity and *c* is a screw for mounting the drawer slide. At least three screws should be used for short drawer slides and, for longer slides, one screw should be placed near each

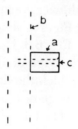

Fig. 6.6. A drawer slide for use where the wall of the cavity is flush with the edge of the drawer opening.

end and the other screws should be spaced about 4 inches apart. For small light drawers, No. 6 screws are adequate but, if the drawer is heavy, No. 8 screws are preferable. The screws should be long enough to go at least 1/2 inch into the wall.

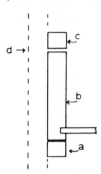

Fig. 6.7. Arrangement of a drawer slide, the side of the drawer and the top guide for the drawer.

It is necessary to have guides for the tops of the drawers to prevent them from tilting down when they are open. Figure 6.7 shows the arrangement of the drawer slide, the side of the drawer and the top guide on one side, where *a* is the drawer slide, *b* is the side of the drawer, *c* is the top guide and *d* is the wall of the drawer cavity. If drawers are arranged, one above another, the slide for one drawer can serve as the top guide for the drawer below it. It will still be necessary to install a special top guide for the top drawer.

6.5. Drawer Stops

Many types of cabinet construction are such that either the back of the drawer front or a lip on the drawer front will serve as a stop for the drawer. There are, however, instances where a flush surface drawer will not be stopped by the drawer front. In these instances, it is necessary to provide stops at the back of the drawer. These stops can take the form of wood blocks glued to the drawer slide or even blocks cut to the proper thickness and glued to the back of the cabinet. The stops should be glued to the slides or to the back of the cabinet so that the drawer will be stopped with its front flush with the face of the cabinet.

7
Work Benches and Shop Cabinets

7.1. Work Benches

If you have a workshop it will be necessary to have some sort of work bench. In a modest shop, a single bench five or six feet long may be sufficient to meet your needs. However, if you have a lathe and a bench mounted drill press, a considerably longer bench will be needed and it may be desirable to have a long bench for the lathe and drill press with a work space at one end and, if space permits, another small bench with a woodworking vise can be an added convenience.

A common type of construction utilizes 4 x 4 inch fir wood legs, 32 inches long, with cross bracing as indicated in Fig. 7.1. The distance between legs in the pair will depend on the width of the top. If 10 inch planks are used for the top, three planks will provide a width of 28 1/2 inches and the width x in Fig. 7.1 should be about 25 inches to allow an overhang along the front. If three 12 inch planks are to be used for the top the distance x in Fig. 7.1 should be about 31 inches.

Pairs of legs like those shown in Fig. 7.1 should be placed at 4 to 6 ft. intervals along the length of the bench with

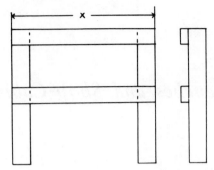

Fig. 7.1. Construction of a pair of wooden legs for supporting a work bench.

a pair placed about 10 or 12 inches from each end. Two by four crossbeams should be attached from the front to the back legs as indicated in Fig. 7.1. The 2 x 4 crossbeams may be nailed to the legs with *12 d* nails but the unit will remain more rigid if they are attached with 2 1/2 inch No. 10 screws because nails tend to work loose in time.

The top should be made from 2 inch fir planks. Three 10 inch planks will provide a width of 28 1/2 inches for the top and three 12 inch planks will provide a width of 34 1/2 inches. In order to provide end to end stiffness, 1 x 10 inch boards should be nailed to the front and back surfaces of the legs with the top edges of the boards flush with the tops of the legs. These boards should be of the same length as the planks used for the top and the ends of the boards should be even with the ends of the top planks. These side boards should be nailed to the legs with three or four *8 d* nails at each leg. The rear top plank should have its edge flush with the outside surface of the rear side board and there will then be some overhang of the top at the front.

The top planks should be nailed to the 2 x 4's at the top of the legs with *10 d* nails. These nails should be driven

The space to the right of the drill press is open work
e with a vise located over pier *D*.

Cabinets Under the Work Bench

e space under a work bench is essentially waste space
has a tendency to collect junk and dirt. A method of
ting for this is to enclose the space and make it into
cabinets. The design of the cabinets will depend on
ture of the things which you need to store in them
e kind of work bench under which it is housed. In
stances it is more desirable to divide the space into
ient widths, much as the space in a lower kitchen
is divided, and install shelves and hang doors on the
may be desirable to install drawers, similar to the
cabinet drawers, under a part of the bench. You
rovide a toe space like that under a lower kitchen
to make it easier to work at the bench.
bench is constructed with wooden legs like those
.1, the 2 x 4 inch crossbeams can be used for sup-
helves. The bottom shelf should be mounted above
by the width of a 2 x 4 (3 1/2 inches) and the
hich support the bottom shelf should be about 3
rter than the width *x* in Fig. 7.1 to provide a toe
els about 8 inches wide, extending from the bot
1 x 10 inch board which extends the length of the
the top of the legs, to the bottom edge of the
lf should be nailed to the front legs so they extend
inches on each side of the leg as indicated in Fig
of doors can be hung from the panels nailed t
or catches similar to those used on kitchen cab
hould be used to hold the doors shut.
desirable to install a drawer in the board whic

down so that their heads do not project above the top surface
of the planks. Three nails should be used at each 2 x 4.

In order to provide a smooth hard working surface on the
top of the bench, the top should be covered with 1/8 inch
tempered hardboard. This surface does not require any kind
of finish and it will last for many years of hard use. The
hardboard sheets should be cut to exactly the same width
as the top and, if the bench is more than 8 ft. long, more
than one sheet will be required. The hardboard can be held
in place with a few 3/4 inch brads driven through it into
the fir planks and slightly countersunk.

It is possible to purchase steel bench legs and bench tops
made from a chipboard core with tempered hardboard on
both sides. These materials are satisfactory for constructing
small work benches. The method of assembly will, of course,
depend on the nature of the particular components purchased.

The benches described above are not very rigid and will
tend to vibrate if a lathe or drill press is mounted on them.
I prefer a bench mounted on concrete block piers. Such a
bench is very rigid and it is no more expensive to construct
than one with wood or steel legs. It is, of course, not
advisable to use concrete block piers unless the shop is in
a basement or outbuilding with a concrete floor. The piers
should be about 6 feet apart and each pier will require six
8 x 8 x 16 inch concrete blocks and four 8 x 8 x 8 inch
concrete blocks. Two of the 8 x 8 x 8 inch blocks and two
of the 8 x 8 x 16 inch blocks should have flat finished ends
in order to provide a pier with a finished front. Mortar for
laying the blocks can be purchased ready mixed in bags
from your building supply dealer so that it is simply necessary to add water to the mortar-mix and mix it when you
are ready to construct the piers.

The blocks should be layed as indicated in Fig. 7.2. You

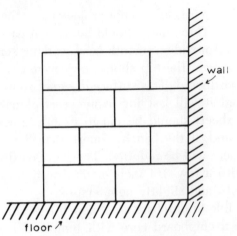

Fig. 7.2. Method of laying concrete blocks for a concrete block
pier to support a work bench.

will need a small trowel to spread the mortar on the surfaces of the blocks where they join together. The pier
shown in Fig. 7.2 will be 32 inches high and 32 inches from
front to back.

The cement blocks are hollow and you can provide a
means for anchoring the top planks to the piers if you wedge
a piece of board in the hollow and fill the space above it
with mortar so that a piece of 2 inch plank will float on
the mortar with its top flush with the top of the pier. You
can provide a support for the board at the bottom of the
mortar by sticking some 10 d nails into the mortar below
the top block before it sets. Figure 7.3 shows a cross section
of a block in the top row where *a* is the concrete block, *b b*
are the pieces of board for holding the mortar, *c c* is the
mortar, *b′ b′* are the pieces of 2 inch plank floated on the
mortar and *d d* are the 12 d nails which are driven about

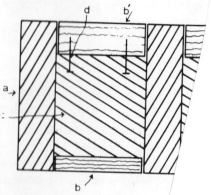

Fig. 7.3. Method of providing a
the bench to the piers

one inch into the 2 inch piec
extend down into the morta
ber to the mortar. When th
on the bench can be attac

I have a workbench 18
The bench is supported by
The end of the bench at
to the concrete block w
The lathe is mounted
maximum stability and

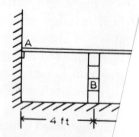

Fig. 7.4. A work b

C.
spa

7.2.

Th
which
corre
usefu
the n
and t
some
conver
cabine
front. I
kitchen
should
cabinet
If the
in Fig. 7
porting s
the floor
2 x 4's w
inches sh
space. Pa
tom of the
bench at
bottom sh
about two
7.5. A pair
the legs. D
inet doors s
It is ofte

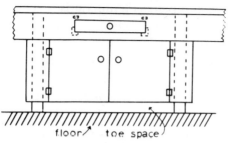

Fig. 7.5. Cabinet space and drawer in a section of bench between two pairs of wooden legs.

runs lengthwise at the top. A rectangular opening of the size desired for the drawer should be cut in the board and drawer slides and guides should be fabricated with a length accurately equal to x in Fig. 7.1 can be attached by nailing through the boards at the front and back. Since it is not practical to make a drawer so deep that it extends to the back of the bench when closed, it will be necessary to install stops on the drawer guides. Top guides, as indicated in Chapter 6, should be installed in a manner similar to the installation of the slides and side guides.

If the work bench is constructed on concrete block piers, it will be necessary to construct a wooden frame to slide into the space between the piers to support the shelves. In order to hang the doors, plywood panels can be attached to the fronts of the piers using lead anchors and screws. The holes for the lead anchors should be drilled in the concrete blocks with a 1/4 inch masonry drill. Three lead anchors with 1 3/4 inch No. 8 screws are adequate to hold the panels. The concrete block piers are 8 inches wide and the width of the panels can be made 12 inches so that they overlap the spaces 2 inches. Of course, the frame for supporting the shelves should be put in place before the panels are installed on the fronts of the piers. Figure 7.6 is a suggested design for a cabinet between two piers six feet between centers. The frame should be constructed of 2 x 4 inch structural lumber and the shelves, panels on the fronts of the piers and the doors can be cut from fir plywood or chipboard. It is desirable to have a strip *a* along the top, which can be attached at the ends to the panels attached to the fronts of the piers with glue blocks and strip *b* can be attached to strip *a* by means of a glue block and it can be attached to the fronts of the shelves with screws or nails. If the space between centers of the piers is six feet and the strip *b* is 2 inches wide and the panels *c* are 12 inches wide the doors will be 14 1/2 inches wide which is a convenient width. The doors can be hung with simple strap hinges and door catches similar to those used on kitchen cabinets are satisfactory. Simple wood door knobs are adequate for such cabinets. The 2 x 4 inch lumber used for supporting the bottom shelf should be cut about 3 inches shorter than the width of the shelf to provide the toe space and the back of the toe space

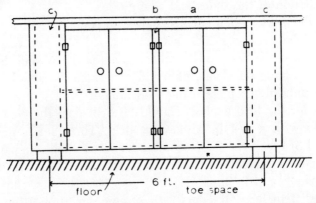

Fig. 7.6. Design of a cabinet space between two concrete block piers.

can be covered with a strip of 1/4 inch plywood. It is not necessary to paint the cabinet but paint will improve its appearance.

7.3. Cigar Box Cabinets

Cigar boxes have long been used as holders of small tools, screws, tacks, brads, nails and other small items of stock which should be available in the chop. If these cigar boxes are not organized, you can spend much time looking for an item. I have found cigar boxes very useful in the shop. Although these boxes are now made of paper, they are surprisingly durable. I have built a cigar box cabinet which is on my work bench primarily for holding small tools. The cabinet contains 18 cigar boxes and it is constructed as indicated in Fig. 7.7. The ends and top are 1/2 inch lumber and the two center columns are 3/4 inch lumber. The shelves are 1/8 inch hardboard and 1/8 inch slots 1/4 inch deep are cut in the vertical columns to receive the ends of the shelves. The width of the columns and shelves is equal to the width of the cigar boxes and the length of the shelves is equal to the length of the cigar boxes plus about 5/8 inch since 1/4 inch at each end of a shelf projects into the slots in the vertical columns. The distance between shelves is about 1/8 inch greater than the height of a cigar box.

In order to make it easier to remove the boxes from the cabinet, small wooden drawer pulls should be installed at the center of the front of each box. White paper should be glued to the fronts of the boxes to provide space for noting the contents of the boxes. If each box is always kept in the same place you will soon be able to always reach for the correct box. Such a simple cabinet is as effective as one constructed with wooden drawers. If one of the cigar

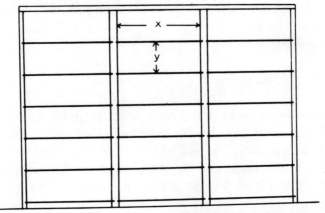

Fig. 7.7. Suggested design of a cigar box cabinet.

boxes becomes damaged it is a simple matter to replace it. However, I have used such a cabinet for at least five years and I have never had to replace a box.

Since I keep a variety of stock such as various sizes of upholstering tacks, various sizes of nails, brads and screws, I have a cigar box cabinet similar to the one shown in Fig. 7.7 which covers the entire end of the work bench extending from the floor to the top of the bench. This would not be a convenient place for keeping small tools to be used when working at the bench but it is very convenient as a place to keep supplies which I like to keep on hand.

8
Special Cabinets

8.1. Introduction

There are many kinds of cabinets which may be constructed for special purposes. For example, if you have a large bedroom closet, it is sometimes desirable to build a cabinet in the closet to serve as a dresser. Such a cabinet will usually have only drawers but there may be some instances where it will be desirable to have a portion at the bottom of the cabinet fitted with doors, which can serve as a storage compartment for shoes.

It should be made from white pine plywood so that it can be painted to match the woodwork in the closet. The drawers and the front frame around the drawers can be made from white pine lumber. The drawers should be constructed and fitted according to the methods described in Chapter 6.

A storage cabinet of fir plywood or chipboard to store items in a garage or basement should be designed, whenever feasible, to utilize the material as efficiently as possible. For example, such material is supplied in 4 x 8 ft. sheets. If the depth of the cabinet can be so designed that the sheets can be divided into three or four equal widths, taking into account the wastage due to the saw cuts, when cutting the ends and the shelves, there will be a minimum of waste. If, then, the width of the cabinet can be made 4 ft., the full width of the sheet used for the back can be used.

8.2. Special Basement Storage Cabinets

Everyone has a number of bulky, seldom used items which may be stored in a basement. It is important to protect such items from dust and dirt so some sort of enclosure such as a cabinet should be provided to protect them. Cabinets made from plywood or chipboard are not inexpensive to construct and the volume of cabinet space required is often quite large. An arrangement which is much less expensive than conventional cabinet construction can be built along a basement wall.

Such a cabinet can be constructed on a framework of 2 x 4 structural lumber. To do this, one 2 x 4 should be attached to the floor along the wall and another along the line of the front of the cabinet. Screws and lead anchors may be used for attaching the 2 x 4's to the floor. Two by four uprights, about three or four feet apart should be nailed to the bottom 2 x 4's and to the ceiling joists. At the levels of the shelves, horizontal 1 x 2 inch strips should be nailed to the vertical 2 x 4's. The shelves can be made of any inexpensive lumber and it is desirable to put the shelves in place before the cabinet is enclosed. Plaster board should be nailed to the ceiling joists over the cabinet to prevent dust from getting into the cabinet from the top.

To enclose the cabinet, a 1 x 4 inch strip should be nailed along the top, and 1 x 4 inch vertical strips should be attached to the vertical 2 x 4's at the front. The doors will be hung from these strips.

In order to save cost in the construction of the doors, they can be made with panels of 1/2 inch plaster board surrounded by a 1 x 4 inch frame of lumber as indicated in

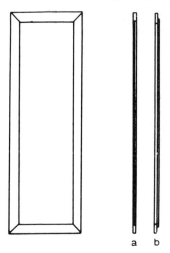

a   b

Fig. 8.1. Panelled door for a basement storage space. *a* shows installation of the panel in a dado cut in the door frame. *b* shows the panel mounted on the back of the door frame when means are not available for cutting dadoes.

Fig. 8.1. A dado, 1/2 inch by 1/2 inch, can be cut on the back edge of the four strips used to make the door frame so that the panels will fit into them as indicated at *a* in Fig. 8.1. However, if you do not have the means to cut the dadoes, the panels can be nailed to the backs of the door frames as indicated at *b* in Fig. 8.1.

A pair of doors can be hung between each pair of vertical 1 x 4 inch strips as shown in Fig. 8.2. Door catches can be installed on the doors to hold them shut and wooden knobs can be installed on the doors for opening them. If the ends of the cabinet terminate at walls, the walls can serve to close the ends. However, if the ends need to be closed, they can be closed with plaster board.

8.3. A Darkroom Cabinet

Many people are amateur photographers and wish to have a place to develop films and make photographic prints. It is awkward to do such work at the kitchen sink or in the bathroom and it is quite expensive to build a darkroom. A darkroom will need to be about 8 x 8 ft. to provide sufficient work space and also, many people do not have the space available to build such a darkroom.

I was faced with the space problem because I needed the space in my basement, not used for storage, for my shop. It occurred to me that I could have the darkroom space without robbing much space from the shop. It was possible

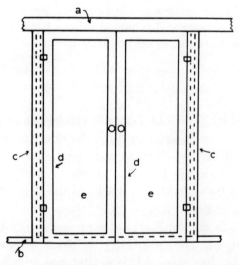

Fig. 8.2. A pair of doors on a basement storage cabinet. *a* is the strip along the top. *b* is the 2 x 4 along the floor at the front of the cabinet. *c* are the vertical 1 x 4 inch strips nailed to the vertical 2 x 4's. *d* are the wood door frames. *e* are the plaster board panels.

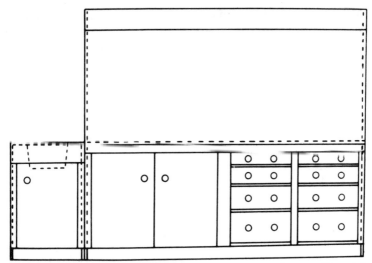

Fig. 8.3. Front of a photographic dark room cabinet. The sink
is in a cabinet at the left.

to put shutters at the basement windows so that the entire
basement could be darkened and the actual counter space
required is about 7 ft. by 20 inches.

I had the counter prepared by my building materials
supplier. He cut a piece of plywood 7 ft. by 20 inches and
cemented white formica to the top and front edge. I then
constructed a cabinet like that in Fig. 8.3. Two tiers of
drawers were built under the counter on the right hand side
and the space under the left hand side is shelf space, enclosed by doors, for storing bottles of processing solutions.
The enlarger is located at the right hand end of the counter
and the processing trays are arranged along the counter
with the print washing tray at the extreme left. Water from
the faucet at the sink is led by rubber tubing to the print
washing tray and the overflow outlet from the tray is led
from the tray to the sink.

When the darkroom space is not in use, a door hinged at the top is closed down to enclose the counter and the space above it to keep sawdust out of the photographic work space. The back of the cabinet is enclosed with 1/4 inch plywood.

Figure 8.4 shows the details of the drawer section which serves as the support for one end of the counter. The front of the drawer section is shown in Fig. 8.4. The rear of this

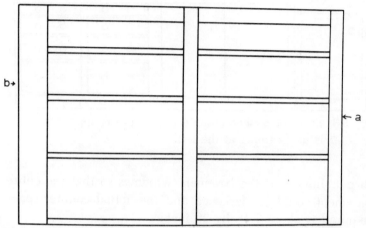

Fig. 8.4. Frame for the drawers below the counter of the photographic darkroom cabinet.

section is identical to the front, and the drawer guides and slides join the front section to the back section. This unit was constructed and mounted on 2 x 4's on the floor in the same manner as the lower cabinet of a kitchen cabinet, leaving a toe space at the front. The strips between the drawers are 3/4 inch wide and two inches deep. The strip below the bottom drawer is 8 inches deep to provide an adequate overlap on the supporting 2 x 4's. The vertical strip *a* overlaps the side of the cabinet and is nailed to it. One of the

doors for the left hand side of the lower cabinet is hung
from the vertical strip b and the support for one end of the
shelf in the left hand cabinet is mounted between the strip
b and the corresponding one at the back.

The ends of the cabinet are cut from 3/4 inch plywood
as indicated in Fig. 8.5. The door which closes the portion
of the cabinet above the counter is indicated at a. This door
is hinged at the top and when it is open it is supported by
means of a hook suspended from the ceiling. This door is
shown in the open position by the dotted lines.

The side of the cabinet is nailed to the end of the counter
at b, and c shows where the side is cut back so that the
drawer fronts will be set back 1 inch from the front edge
of the counter. The cutout at d is for the purpose of provid-

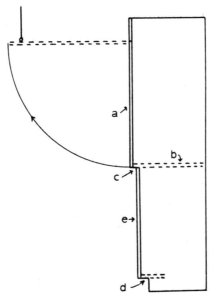

Fig. 8.5. End view of the photographic dark room cabinet.

ing the toe space at the front of the cabinet. The strip *a* in Fig. 8.4 is nailed to the front edge of the side at *e* in Fig. 8.5.

By means of this cabinet it is possible to have an adequate photographic work space with a loss of only about 15 square feet from the shop space. If you construct such a cabinet, the actual length should depend on the counter space which you will require. I constructed my cabinet with the sink on the outside because I needed to have access to the sink when the cabinet is closed. If this is not necessary, it would be more convenient to have the sink enclosed within the cabinet. See Section 3.7 for the method of incorporating the sink in a counter top.

8.4. A Sewing Work Space

Many housewives do considerable sewing but do not have a room available which can be set aside as a sewing room. When the sewing must be done in a room used for other purposes, it is often necessary to spend considerable time to get the materials out to start work and then gather them all up and put them away at the end of a session.

It is possible to construct a space at the end of a room which can house a sewing machine and all of the materials involved in sewing. A sewing machine head can be mounted on a swingout shelf with the same hardware as is used for a mixer shelf. A main shelf can be installed at standard counter height and the swingout shelf for the sewing machine can be mounted under it. A set of drawers similar to those shown in Fig. 8.4 can be constructed to go on each side of the space for the swingout shelf for the sewing machine and the frames for these drawers can serve as the support for the main shelf. Shelves for holding the sewing materials can be installed above the main shelf.

The sewing center will need to be at least 15 inches deep

Fig. 8.6. Sewing center with the doors open and the sewing machine in operating position.

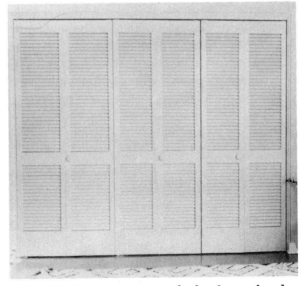

Fig. 8.7. Sewing center with the doors closed.

in order to accommodate the swingout shelf for the sewing machine. The entire sewing center can be enclosed with standard folding doors which operate on floor and ceiling tracks.

When sewing is to be done, the doors are pushed open and the sewing machine can be swung out into its operating position. When the room is to be used for another purpose, the materials can be put on the shelves, the sewing machine folded down to its storage position and the doors closed.

Figure 8.6 shows such a sewing center with the doors open and the sewing machine in operating position. Figure 8.7 shows the sewing center with the doors closed, hiding the sewing machine and the shelves and drawers. The doors used in the sewing center shown in Figs. 8.6 and 8.7 are louvered doors, however any type of standard door which blends with the other woodwork in the room can be used. Such a sewing center can be constructed using approximately 18 inches at the end of the room.

The problem of installing the doors may be beyond the competence of many amateurs. However, the sewing center can be constructed and a professional carpenter can be called in to install the doors. It is also advisable to have an electrician install an electrical outlet for the sewing machine in the back of the space where the sewing machine folds and he can also install a fluorescent light under a shelf above the machine to provide illumination while sewing.

9
Bookshelves

9.1. Introduction

Bookshelves are constructed in a large variety of sizes and shapes. Small bookshelves may be movable from place to place in a room and the larger ones are usually built in place and therefore constitute a part of the woodwork in the room. The load carried by a bookshelf can be quite heavy. I weighed the books from a representative shelf 36 inches long and found that they weighed 45 pounds. Because of the heaviness of books, bookshelves must be strong, and it is not advisable to have the span of shelves much more than three feet unless additional support is provided at the center of the shelf. Although bookshelves are often constructed from 8 inch lumber, which would provide shelves 7 1/2 inches deep, it is much better practice to use 10 inch lumber to provide shelves 9 1/2 inches deep.

Plywood is stiffer than ordinary lumber so that a shelf made of plywood will have less tendency to sag than one made of lumber. A sagging bookshelf is unattractive, and it tends to pull the structure out of shape in bookcases that have the shelves permanently attached at the ends.

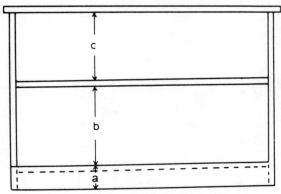

Fig. 9.1. Small two-shelf bookcase.

9.2. *Small Bookcases*

Small bookcases are often constructed for placement under windows. These bookcases are not usually built in place, but there are some instances where they are permanently built in. Such bookcases often have two shelves. Figure 9.1 shows an example of such a bookcase. The dimension *a* should be about 3 inches. It is often made the same width as the baseboards around the room. The dimensions *b* and *c* will usually be approximately 11 and 9 inches respectively but will depend on the heights of books to be stored on the bookshelf.

There is no problem in adequately supporting the bottom shelf because the strip of lumber covering the space *a* can be nailed to the front edge of the shelf. The problem of supporting the middle shelf is not so simple. If the shelf is simply supported by nails driven through the end pieces, the entire weight of the shelf and its load of books will have to be carried by these nails. An improved method for supporting such intermediate shelves is to cut a dado across

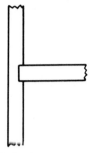

Fig. 9.2. Use of a dado to support the end of a shelf.

the end pieces as indicated in Fig. 9.2. The dado should be cut about 1/4 inch deep and its width should be such that the end of the shelf will fit snugly into it.

If you have a power saw, it is a simple matter to cut the dado, but it can be formed by cutting two slots with a hand saw and removing the wood between the cuts with a chisel.

An alternate method of supporting intermediate shelves, which may be used on small bookshelves but is more com-

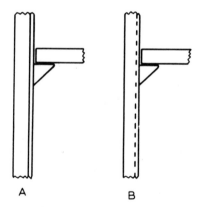

A   B

Fig. 9.3. Methods of attaching pilaster standards to the bookshelf vertical members.

monly used on larger bookshelves, is the use of pilaster standards and brackets. The pilaster standards can be cut to any desired length from stock obtainable from building supply dealers. The stock is in the form of a channel 5/8 inch wide and 3/16 inch thick with rectangular notches cut at 1/2 inch intervals. Brackets, for supporting the shelves, are available which fit into the notches on the standards. When these standards are used, they are attached to the ends of the bookcases with their centers about 1 1/2 inches from the front and back edges. The standards can be attached to the surfaces of the ends of the cabinet, but a neater job will result if dadoes in which the standards can be countersunk are cut 5/8 inch wide and 3/16 inch deep. Figure 9.3 shows an end of a shelf supported by pilaster standards and brackets. A standard attached to the surface is shown at *A* and a countersunk standard is shown at *B*. Small bookcases should always have backs which may be made of 1/4 inch plywood or 1/8 inch hardboard. The back serves to keep dust out of the bookshelves and it also serves to strengthen the structure.

9.3. Large Bookshelves

Large bookshelves are built-in; that is, they are permanently anchored in place. Sometimes such bookshelves are made to have shelves from floor to ceiling with the bottom shelf arranged in a manner similar to that in Fig. 9.1. Vertical uprights should be spaced at intervals of approximately 3 feet and not more than 4 feet. In most instances, the uprights which support the shelves are equally spaced but there are some instances where the design is more interesting if the uprights are not equally spaced.

Pilaster standards and brackets should always be used

Fig. 9.4. A large bookshelf with a cupboard at the bottom.

on large bookshelves. If the bookshelf is quite large you can take the uprights to a lumber mill to have the dadoes cut for the pilaster standards if you do not have a power saw with a dado cutter.

Often, large bookshelves are constructed with cupboard space at the bottom. Shelves near the floor are inconvenient for storing books and there are many things, including some books, which are more conveniently kept in a cupboard with doors at the front. Usually, such a cupboard space is made to be deeper than the bookshelves. Figure 9.4 shows a cross-section of a bookshelf with a cupboard below it. The shelf *a* should be a 12 inch board and the widths of the bookshelves should be 10 inches. If the shelf space is quite large, the appearance of the unit will be enhanced if 1 1/8 inch lumber is used for the shelf *a*, while 3/4 inch lumber is used for the rest of the structure.

In cases where a set of bookshelves is constructed along

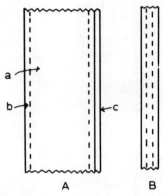

Fig. 9.5. Construction of a wide column for supporting shelves in a bookcase.

the entire length and height of the end of a room, vertical uprights made of a single thickness of 3/4 inch lumber tend to look flimsy, and, indeed, they are flimsy.

A more substantial kind of upright can be fabricated like that shown in Fig. 9.5. Two 1 x 10 inch boards of the proper length are nailed together with 3/4 x 3/4 inch strips along the edges between them. A side view is indicated at *A*, where a 1 x 10 inch board is indicated at *a* and the 3/4 x 3/4 inch strips are indicated at *b*. The thickness of the column will be 2 1/4 inches and the front of the column is covered with a 3/4 x 2 1/4 inch strip. The front edge of the column is

Fig. 9.6. Floor-to-ceiling bookshelves covering an entire wall of a study.

shown at *B* in Fig. 9.5. Figure 9.6 shows a set of bookshelves made with columns like those shown in Fig. 9.5.

It is necessary to consider the finishing of the tops of large bookshelves. This is similar to the problem of finishing the tops of upper kitchen cabinets. In some instances, large bookshelves will be built to the level of window and door fraames and in others they will extend to the ceiling. If a molding is consistent with the other woodwork trim in the room, such a molding along the top edge of the bookshelf may be appropriate. In some instances, in modern houses, a simple quarter round molding at the top of a

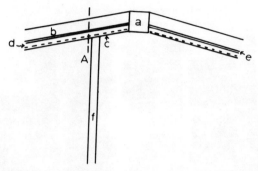

Fig. 9.7. Front view showing the method of finishing off the top of the bookshelves shown in Fig. 9.6.

bookshelf which extends to the ceiling may be the most satisfactory way of finishing the top.

The bookshelves shown in Fig. 9.6 are built along the entire wall of a study that has beamed cathedral ceilings. Figure 9.7 shows a portion of the top of the bookshelf to indicate the method of finishing it. The central beam *a*, which runs perpendicular to the bookshelves, extends about 2 inches below the other beams. A beam *b* at the end of the room runs parallel and directly over the bookshelves. At the top of the bookshelves, against which the tops of the col-

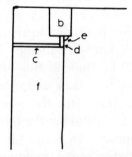

Fig. 9.8. Cross section of the view shown in Fig. 9.7.

umns are attached (shown at c and d), is a finish strip to
extend from the bottom of c to the bottom of the beam b.
A quarter round molding e is nailed in the corner formed
by the junction of d with the beam b and f is one of the
vertical columns for supporting the shelves. Figure 9.8 shows
a cross section at A of Fig. 9.7. The beam over the bookshelf
is at b; c is the top of the bookshelf; d is the finish strip between the top and the beam; and e is the quarter round
between d and b. The vertical column f in Fig. 9.7 is also
indicated at f in Fig. 9.8.

When our house was built, the beam b was, of course,
installed by the carpenters. When the finishing work was
being done, I constructed the bookshelves, and the strip d
and the quarter round e served to tie the bookshelves to the
carpenter's finish work.

When building large bookshelves in a room, you should
carefully consider the way in which you will finish the top.
No rules can be established for this, as it is important
that such bookshelves look as though they belong in the
room. The other woodwork and your good taste should dic-
tate how this should be done. You can get helpful ideas by
looking at pictures in magazines. If you are building a new
house and have an architect, he can be very helpful in working out designs.

10
Finishing Cabinets

10.1. Enamel Finish

Cabinets made from white pine lumber or plywood should be painted if they are located in a part of the home where a finish is required. We now have a great variety of colors of enamels available and they are available in glossy, semi-gloss and flat finish.

Before starting to finish a cabinet you should inspect all of the surfaces, and sand down any rough places, and be certain that all nails are set so that putty can be filled in over their heads. All corners should be sanded so that they are slightly rounded. All plywood edges which show should be covered with veneer tape. This tape is paper backed and can be glued to the edge of the plywood with contact cement. The tape is wider than the plywood and can be trimmed back flush with the plywood with a sharp knife or a razor blade after the cement has set. Do not round the edges of the plywood before applying wood veneer tape. When the tape has been trimmed the edges should then be slightly rounded.

The first coat of paint should always be an enamel under-coat. This is a special paint which penetrates the wood and provides a good surface for the enamel. When the enamel undercoat has dried over night, the surface will feel slightly rough because the grain of the wood is slightly raised. You should rub the entire surface lightly with steel wool or fine sandpaper to provide a smooth surface for the enamel. This is very important. A smooth enamel surface is easy to wash but, if you apply enamel over an enamel undercoat which has not been sanded or rubbed with steel wool you will always have a rough surface.

After the enamel undercoat has been rubbed down with steel wool or fine sandpaper, fill the nail holes with putty and apply the first coat of enamel with either a good bristle brush or a roller. If you use a paint roller there will still be many parts of a cabinet where the roller cannot be used. I prefer to use a brush for the entire job.

You can do a reasonably good job with one coat of enamel over the enamel undercoat, but the job will be better if you apply two coats of the enamel.

When you select the color of the enamel you wish to use, the paint dealer will probably need to mix the pigments to produce the desired color. You should be certain to have enough enamel mixed to do the entire job. If you must go back for a second batch of enamel it may not match the first batch exactly.

If you are using a hardwood plywood for the outside of the cabinets which will have their natural finish instead of being painted, the inside of the cabinet and the inside of all drawers should be painted in order to make the surfaces easy to clean.

Although basement cabinets are usually not painted, shop cabinets should be painted so that any oil dropped on the surface can be wiped off. Photographic darkroom cabinets will soon become badly stained with photographic processing solutions if they are not painted.

10.2. Stain

If you have used a hardwood plywood such as birch you may wish to stain it before applying the final finish. You can purchase oil stain of the desired color and apply it with a brush and rub it down with a cloth. If one application does not darken the wood sufficiently, a second coat can be applied. Nail holes can be filled with putty sticks of the desired color.

If a cabinet or bookshelf is constructed of a dark hardwood and it is necessary to use white pine molding at the top, it will be necessary to stain the molding to match the hardwood surface of the plywood.

10.3. Sealer Fnish

Sealer is usually used to finish hardwood plywood cabinets. You can purchase wood veneer tape to match any of the hardwood plywoods for covering the edges. The tape should be applied with contact cement. Any stain should be allowed to dry overnight and the nail holes should be filled using the properly colored putty stick.

The sealer should be applied with a good bristle brush and after the first coat has dried overnight, the entire surface should be lightly sanded with fine sandpaper before applying the second coat. Two coats of sealer are sufficient to provide a good finish.

Index

109